Welcome to the Heart Healthy Cookbook for Beginners, when  ook is designed to help you create mouthwatering meals that are both sat _____ ed with flavorful recipes and valuable tips, it is your go-to guide for embracin_____

Inside, you'll find a diverse range of recipes carefully crafted to be low in saturated fats, _____ ____ olesterol while rich in essential nutrients. From hearty salads to comforting soups, and from flavorful seafood dishes to wholesome vegetarian meals, we've got you covered with dishes that will tantalize your taste buds and nourish your heart.

Each recipe in this cookbook includes detailed nutritional information, making it easier to make informed choices about your meals. Please note, the information provided is for educational purposes only and is not intended as medical advice. It is not a substitute for professional medical diagnosis, treatment, or dietary guidance. Always seek the advice of your physician or qualified healthcare provider regarding any medical condition or nutritional changes.

The recipes in this cookbook are designed to promote heart health by incorporating ingredients beneficial for cardiovascular wellness. However, individual nutritional needs may vary. It is essential to consult with a healthcare professional or registered dietitian if you have specific dietary requirements, food allergies, or medical conditions.

While every effort has been made to ensure the accuracy of the nutritional information provided for each recipe, variations in ingredients, cooking methods, and portion sizes may affect the final dietary content.

The information provided in this book, Heart Healthy Cookbook for Beginners, is for educational and informational purposes only and is not intended as medical advice. This book is not a substitute for professional medical treatment or diagnosis. Always seek the advice of your physician or other qualified health providers with any questions you may have regarding a medical condition, particularly if you have heart problems or are at risk for heart disease.

Individual nutritional needs can vary, and the dietary changes suggested may not be suitable for everyone. It is important to consult with a healthcare professional before making any significant changes to your diet, especially if you have underlying health conditions.

By using this book, you acknowledge and agree that neither the author nor the publisher has any liability to you or any other person for any loss, damage, or injury caused or alleged to be caused directly or indirectly by any dietary or lifestyle changes made in reliance on the information contained in this book.

For any medical concerns, please consult a qualified healthcare professional. Use nutritional information as a general guideline and adjust based on individual dietary goals and needs. Cooking and eating habits are personal choices, and individuals are responsible for making informed decisions about their health and wellness.

CONTENTS

Chapter 1
Heart Healthy Eating. Nourishing Your Cardiovascular Well-Being

1.1 Defining the Significance of Caring for Heart Health through Proper Nutrition

An the intricate tapestry of well-being, the heart stands as the orchestrator of vitality, dictating the ebb and flow of life within us. In the symphony of our well-being, the heart plays a central and indispensable role, pumping life through the intricate network of our circulatory system. As we delve into the realms of heart healthy eating it becomes paramount to lay the foundation by understanding the profound significance of caring for heart health through the lens of proper nutrition.

Our dietary choices are not mere fuel for our bodies; they serve as the building blocks for the intricate machinery that is the cardiovascular system. The heart, a resilient yet delicate organ, relies heavily on the nutrients we provide it. Essential vitamins, minerals, and antioxidants act as the sustenance that fuels its rhythmic contractions and ensures the smooth flow of blood.

Caring for our heart transcends the simplistic notion of calorie counting. It involves a holistic approach to nutrition considering the quality of our food rather than merely its quantity.

Understanding the profound significance of caring for heart health through proper nutrition is not just a matter of physical well-being; it is a fundamental investment in the essence of life itself.

At the very core of our being, the heart stands as an unsung hero, orchestrating the symphony of life. Its health is not a trivial matter but the linchpin on which our overall well-being pivots. Recognizing the pivotal role of the heart prompts a deeper understanding of how the choices we make in the realm of nutrition play a fundamental role in fortifying its resilience.

Proper nutrition is not a mere afterthought; it is the architect of cardiovascular resilience. The nutrients we ingest become the building blocks for a heart that beats with vitality. A balanced and thoughtful diet ensures that the heart receives the essential vitamins, minerals, and antioxidants it requires to function optimally. It's not just about eating; it's about providing the heart with the tools it needs to navigate the complexities of life within us.

Armed with knowledge, individuals are not just passive consumers of food; they become active participants in their heart's well-being. The choices made at the dining table transform from mere preferences to conscious commitments to enduring health. Defining the significance of caring for heart health through proper nutrition becomes a journey – a journey towards a life rich in vitality, longevity, and the resilient beat of a heart that echoes the symphony of life. It is an investment not just in the physical but in the very essence of our existence.

1.2 Fundamentals of Heart-Healthy Eating

At the heart of heart-healthy eating lies the fundamental concept of balance. A balanced diet ensures that the body receives the right proportion of macronutrients – carbohydrates, proteins, and fats – essential for optimal functioning. Striking this delicate balance supports the heart by maintaining healthy cholesterol levels, regulating blood pressure, and providing sustained energy.

Prioritizing Whole Foods: Nature's Bounty

The cornerstone of heart-healthy eating is the incorporation of whole foods. Fresh fruits, vegetables, whole grains, and lean proteins constitute the foundation of a nutrient-rich diet. These foods are rich in fiber, antioxidants, vitamins, and minerals, providing the heart with the essential elements it needs to thrive. Choosing whole foods over processed alternatives is a fundamental shift towards heart-conscious nutrition.

Healthy Fats: Choosing Wisely for Cardiovascular Resilience

Contrary to the outdated notion that all fats are detrimental, heart-healthy eating acknowledges the importance of healthy fats. Unsaturated fats in sources like avocados, nuts, and olive oil support heart health. These fats reduce harmful cholesterol levels while preserving the integrity of cell membranes, promoting overall cardiovascular resilience.

The Role of Omega-3 Fatty Acids: A Heart-Boosting Powerhouse

Omega-3 fatty acids, abundant in fatty fish such as salmon, flaxseeds, and walnuts, emerge as superheroes in heart-healthy nutrition. These essential fats confer numerous cardiovascular benefits, including reducing inflammation, improving blood vessel function, and enhancing overall heart performance. Incorporating omega-3-rich foods is a fundamental step in the journey toward heart well-being.

Mindful Portions: Nourishing Without Overburdening

An awareness of portion sizes is fundamental to heart-healthy eating. Mindful eating involves savoring each bite, recognizing hunger and fullness cues, and avoiding overindulgence. Controlling portion sizes not only aids in weight management but also ensures that the heart receives the necessary nutrients without being burdened by excess calories.

Limiting Sodium Intake: A Salty Affair

Excessive sodium intake has been linked to elevated blood pressure, a significant risk factor for heart disease. The fundamentals of heart-healthy eating involve being mindful of salt consumption. Choosing fresh, whole foods over processed and packaged options and utilizing herbs and spices for flavoring are crucial steps in maintaining optimal sodium levels for heart health.

Hydration: The Unsung Hero of Heart Health

As we delve into the fundamentals, the role of proper hydration emerges as a silent champion in heart-healthy eating. Water aids in digestion supports nutrient absorption and helps maintain blood viscosity. Staying adequately hydrated ensures the heart can efficiently pump blood, contributing to overall cardiovascular well-being.

The fundamentals of heart-healthy eating revolve around balance, whole foods, healthy fats, mindful portions, sodium awareness, and hydration. It's not a restrictive regimen but a sustainable and enjoyable approach to nourishing the heart. By embracing these fundamentals, individuals embark on a journey towards a lifestyle that promotes heart health and enhances overall vitality and well-being.

1.3 Heart-Friendly Foods

A heart-healthy diet is characterized by various nutrient-rich foods that support cardiovascular well-being. Incorporating the following foods into your diet can help establish a heart-protective eating routine:

Fatty Fish: Abundant in omega-3 fatty acids, varieties such as salmon, mackerel, trout, and sardines help decrease triglyceride levels, minimize inflammation, and promote cardiovascular wellness.

Berries: Packed with antioxidants, such as blueberries, strawberries, and raspberries, can help reduce oxidative stress and inflammation.

Oats: High in soluble fiber, oats can help lower cholesterol levels and stabilize blood sugar, promoting heart health.

Nuts and Seeds: Walnuts, almonds, chia seeds, and flaxseeds provide heart-healthy fats, fiber, and antioxidants, making them superb choices for your diet.

Leafy Greens: Spinach, kale, collard greens, and Swiss chard offer a wealth of vitamins, minerals, and antioxidants that promote heart health.

Avocado: Packed with monounsaturated fats, avocados have the potential to reduce unhealthy cholesterol levels and support cardiovascular well-being.

Legumes: Beans, lentils, and chickpeas provide significant fiber, protein, and essential nutrients, contributing to heart health by reducing cholesterol levels.

Whole Grains: Foods like brown rice, quinoa, whole wheat, and oats provide complex carbohydrates, fiber, and nutrients that support heart function.

Tomatoes: Rich in lycopene, tomatoes have been associated with a lower risk of heart disease. Cooking them enhances the availability of this heart-protective compound.

Garlic is known for its potential to lower blood pressure and cholesterol levels but has cardiovascular benefits.

Olive Oil: An essential element of the Mediterranean diet, extra virgin olive oil contains abundant monounsaturated fats and antioxidants, which are beneficial for heart health.

Green Tea: With its high antioxidant content, green tea has been linked to reduced risk factors for heart disease.

Dark Chocolate: In moderation, dark chocolate (with at least 70% cocoa content) contains flavonoids that may have heart-protective effects.

Broccoli and Cruciferous Vegetables: These vegetables are rich in fiber, vitamins, and antioxidants that support heart health.

Fruits high in Potassium: Bananas, oranges, cantaloupe, and kiwi are examples of fruits high in potassium, which helps regulate blood pressure.

Fiber-rich Foods: Foods like beans, lentils, whole grains, and fruits provide soluble fiber that helps lower cholesterol levels.

Fruits with Citrus: Oranges, grapefruits, and lemons are rich in vitamin C and antioxidants, contributing to heart health.

Foods Rich in Magnesium: Spinach, almonds, peanuts, and black beans are high in magnesium, which is essential for heart muscle function.

Low-Fat Dairy: Low-fat or fat-free dairy products provide essential nutrients without excessive saturated fats.

Pomegranate: Pomegranate has antioxidant properties and may help lower blood pressure and reduce inflammation.

Including a range of these food items in your diet and adopting a balanced and attentive nutritional strategy can aid in long-term heart well-being. It's crucial to seek guidance from a healthcare provider or a registered dietitian before making substantial dietary alterations particularly if you have pre-existing health issues.

1.4 Heart Hazards: What to Avoid

Avoiding certain foods and lifestyle choices is crucial for maintaining heart health and preventing cardiovascular issues. Here's a list of heart hazards that should be minimized or eliminated from your diet and daily routine:

Saturated and Trans Fats: Limit intake of foods high in saturated and trans fats, such as red meat, processed meats, full-fat dairy products, and commercially baked goods. These fats can raise harmful cholesterol levels and contribute to heart disease.

Excessive Sodium: High sodium intake can lead to hypertension, a significant risk factor for heart disease. Reduce consumption of processed and packaged foods, and be mindful of added salt when cooking and at the table.

Added Sugars: Excess sugar consumption is linked to obesity, diabetes, and heart disease. Limit intake of sugary beverages, candies, pastries, and processed foods with hidden sugars.

Processed and Fast Foods: These often contain high levels of unhealthy fats, sodium, and added sugars. Opt for fresh, whole foods instead of convenient but nutritionally poor alternatives.

Sugar-Sweetened Beverages: Consuming sugary drinks like sodas and fruit juices increases the risk of heart disease. Choose water, herbal teas, or beverages without added sugars.

Excessive Alcohol: Although moderate alcohol intake might offer certain cardiovascular advantages, excessive consumption can result in elevated blood pressure, cardiomyopathy, and a heightened risk of heart failure. It's recommended to restrict alcohol consumption to moderate levels.

High-Caffeine Energy Drinks: These beverages often contain high levels of caffeine and added sugars, which can negatively impact heart health. Choose alternatives like black coffee or herbal teas.

Processed Meats: Foods like sausages, hot dogs, and bacon are high in saturated fats and sodium. Limit consumption and opt for leaner protein sources like poultry, fish, and plant-based alternatives.

Fried Foods: Fried foods, especially those deep-fried in unhealthy oils, contribute to the intake of trans fats and can raise harmful cholesterol levels.

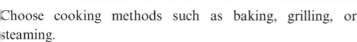

Choose cooking methods such as baking, grilling, or steaming.

Unhealthy Cooking Oils: Avoid using oils high in saturated and trans fats, such as palm and partially hydrogenated oils. Instead, opt for heart-healthy oils like olive, canola, or avocado.

Lack of Physical Activity: Sedentary lifestyles contribute to obesity and cardiovascular risk factors. Consistent exercise is crucial for sustaining optimal heart health.

Smoking: Smoking poses a substantial risk for heart disease by harming blood vessels, reducing oxygen supply to the heart, and aiding in the progression of atherosclerosis. Quitting smoking is a crucial step towards improving heart health.

Stress: Chronic stress can negatively impact heart health. To mitigate its effects, practice stress-management techniques such as meditation, yoga, or deep breathing exercises.

Ignoring Regular Check-ups: Neglecting routine medical check-ups and screenings may result in undetected health issues. Regular monitoring helps identify and address potential heart hazards early on.

By being mindful of these heart hazards and making positive lifestyle changes, individuals can significantly reduce their risk of cardiovascular issues and promote long-term heart health.

1.5 Developing a meal plan to support heart health

Always consult with healthcare professionals for personalized advice based on individual health conditions.

1. Begin with Colorful Fruits and Vegetables: Aim to fill half your plate with various colorful fruits and vegetables. Incorporate a mix of leafy greens, berries, citrus fruits, carrots, and cruciferous vegetables.

2. Embrace Whole Grains: Choose whole grains over refined options to enhance fiber intake. Examples include brown rice, quinoa, whole wheat pasta, oats, and barley.

3. Opt for Lean Proteins: Prioritize lean protein sources such as skinless poultry, fish, legumes, tofu, and beans. Fatty fish like salmon and trout are excellent choices for omega-3 fatty acids.

4. Include Healthy Fats: Eat heart-friendly fats such as avocados, nuts, seeds, and olive oil. Reduce your intake of saturated and trans fats commonly found in processed foods and fried dishes.

5. Mindful Portion Control: Pay attention to portion sizes to prevent overeating. Use smaller plates and bowls to help with portion control.

6. Watch Your Sodium Intake: Limit added salt in cooking and choose low-sodium alternatives. Be cautious of processed foods, as they often contain high sodium levels.

7. Prioritize Omega-3 Fatty Acids: Include sources of omega-3 fatty acids, such as flaxseeds, chia seeds, walnuts, and fatty fish. These fats have anti-inflammatory properties and support heart health.

8. Minimize Added Sugars: Reduce the intake of sugary beverages, candies, and processed sweets. Choose natural sweeteners like honey or opt for desserts with reduced sugar content.

9. Hydrate Wisely: Stay well-hydrated with water throughout the day. Limit the consumption of sugary drinks and excessive caffeine.

10. Balance Your Meals: Strive for a balanced combination of carbohydrates, proteins, and healthy fats in each meal. Include a variety of foods to ensure a broad spectrum of nutrients.

11. Plan Ahead: Prepare meals in advance to avoid reliance on unhealthy, convenient options. Plan a weekly menu and create a shopping list based on heart-healthy ingredients.

12. Minimize Processed Foods: Reduce your intake of processed and packaged foods high in unhealthy fats, sodium, and additives. Choose whole and fresh foods whenever feasible.

13. Cook at Home: Home-cooked meals allow you to control ingredients and cooking methods. Try using herbs and spices to add flavor instead of relying on excessive salt.

14. Choose Heart-Healthy Cooking Methods: Opt for heart-friendly cooking methods like grilling, baking, steaming, and sautéing. Limit deep-frying, as it can introduce unhealthy fats.

15. Enjoy Regular, Balanced Meals: Aim for regular meal times to maintain consistent energy levels. Avoid skipping meals, as it can lead to overeating later on.

16. Be Mindful of Alcohol Consumption: If you consume alcohol, do so in moderation. Limit intake to recommended levels.

17. Explore Heart-Healthy Recipes: Seek out and experiment with recipes designed for heart health. Explore diverse cuisines to keep your meals exciting and enjoyable.

18. Stay Informed and Educated: Stay updated on nutritional guidelines and heart-healthy recommendations. Seek personalized advice from a registered dietitian or healthcare professional.

Creating a heart-healthy meal plan is a proactive step toward nurturing your cardiovascular well-being. By making informed choices and embracing a balanced and diverse approach to nutrition, you can support your heart' health and contribute to a vibrant and energetic life.

1.6 The Role of Physical Activity for Heart Health

Physical activity is pivotal in maintaining cardiovascular health and preventing heart disease. Regular exercise offers many benefits, ranging from improving heart function to managing risk factors associated with cardiovascular issues. Here's an exploration of the crucial role physical activity plays in promoting heart health:

Strengthening the Heart Muscle
Regular exercise, especially aerobic activities like walking, running, and cycling, helps strengthen the heart muscle. A stronger heart can pump blood more efficiently, reducing the strain on the cardiovascular system.

Improving Blood Circulation
Engaging in physical activity boosts blood circulation throughout the body. This improved circulation ensures efficient delivery of oxygen and nutrients to cells, optimizing cardiovascular function.

Lowering Blood Pressure
Exercise is an effective means of reducing high blood pressure, a significant risk factor for heart disease. Regular physical activity promotes more relaxed and flexible blood vessels, contributing to lower blood pressure levels.

Physical activity is pivotal in maintaining cardiovascular health and preventing heart disease. Regular exercise offers many benefits, ranging from improving heart function to managing risk factors associated with cardiovascular issues. Here's an exploration of the crucial role physical activity plays in promoting heart health:

Strengthening the Heart Muscle
Regular exercise, especially aerobic activities like walking, running, and cycling, helps strengthen the heart muscle. A stronger heart can pump blood more efficiently, reducing the strain on the cardiovascular system.

Improving Blood Circulation
Engaging in physical activity boosts blood circulation throughout the body. This improved circulation ensures efficient delivery of oxygen and nutrients to cells, optimizing cardiovascular function.

Lowering Blood Pressure
Exercise is an effective means of reducing high blood pressure, a significant risk factor for heart disease. Regular physical activity promotes more relaxed and flexible blood vessels, contributing to lower blood pressure levels.

Enhancing Cholesterol Profiles
Engaging in regular exercise can help raise high-density lipoprotein (HDL or "good") cholesterol and lower low-density lipoprotein (LDL or "bad") cholesterol levels. This favorable shift in cholesterol profiles reduces the risk of atherosclerosis and heart disease.

Managing Weight
Regular physical activity plays a crucial role in managing weight and preventing obesity. Keeping a healthy weight helps lower the risk of developing conditions such as diabetes and hypertension, which are closely associated with heart disease.

Controlling Blood Sugar Levels
Regular exercise improves insulin sensitivity and helps control blood sugar levels. Managing blood sugar is essential for preventing diabetes, a condition significantly increasing heart disease risk.

Reducing Inflammation
Chronic inflammation is a contributing factor to heart disease. Exercise has anti-inflammatory effects, helping to reduce inflammation throughout the body. This anti-inflammatory action contributes to improved arterial health and decreased risk of cardiovascular issues.

Enhancing Mental Health
Exercise benefits mental well-being, reducing stress, anxiety, and depression. Lowering stress levels positively impacts heart health by reducing the burden on the cardiovascular system.

Promoting Healthy Sleep
Engaging in regular physical activity promotes improved sleep quality. Quality sleep, in turn, is linked to a reduced risk of heart disease and enhanced overall well-being.

Boosting Overall Cardiovascular Resilience
Exercise strengthens the entire cardiovascular system, from the heart to blood vessels. Improved resilience enhances the body's ability to respond to stressors and challenges, promoting long-term heart health.

Encouraging Healthy Lifestyle Choices
Regular physical activity often leads to other healthy lifestyle choices, such as adopting a balanced diet and avoiding harmful habits like smoking. These combined efforts create a comprehensive approach to heart health.

Preventing Sedentary-Related Risks
Sedentary lifestyles are associated with an increased risk of heart disease. Regular physical activity counteracts the negative impact of prolonged sitting and sedentary behavior.

Engaging in a combination of aerobic exercises, strength training, and flexibility exercises is vital to reap the full benefits of physical activity for heart health. The American Heart Association recommends at least 150 minutes of moderate-intensity aerobic exercise or 75 minutes of vigorous-intensity exercise per week, along with muscle-strengthening activities at least two days a week.

Here's a list of simple exercises that can help you stay physically fit:

Walking
·One of the simplest yet effective exercises.
·Aim for at least 30 minutes of brisk walking most days of the week.

Jogging or Running in Place
·Requires minimal space and no equipment.
·Boosts cardiovascular health and burns calories.

Jumping Jacks
·A full-body exercise that elevates heart rate.
·Incorporate them into a quick cardio routine.

Bodyweight Squats
·Strengthens the lower body, including the thighs and glutes.
·Keep your feet shoulder-width apart and squat as if sitting back in a chair.

Push-Ups
·Works the chest, shoulders, and triceps.
·Modify by doing them against a wall or on your knees if needed.

Plank
·Engages the core muscles.
·Hold a plank position, keeping your body straight from head to heels.

Lunges
·Strengthens the legs and glutes.
·Step forward with one foot and lower your body until both knees are bent at a 90-degree angle.

Burpees
·Combines cardio and strength training.
·Involves a series of movements like squatting, jumping, and push-ups.

Bicycle Crunches
·Targets the abdominal muscles.
·Lie on your back, lift your legs, and practice cycling while touching your elbow to the opposite knee.

Tricep Dips
·Works the triceps and back of the arms.
·Use a sturdy chair or bench to dip down and push back up.

Standing Calf Raises
·Strengthens the calf muscles.
·Stand flat, lift your heels, and lower them back down.

Leg Raises
·Targets the lower abdominal muscles.
·Lie on your back and lift your legs upward while keeping them straight.

Yoga or Pilates
·Incorporate simple yoga poses or Pilates exercises for flexibility, balance, and overall body strength.

Jump Rope
·Great for cardiovascular fitness and coordination.
·Start with short intervals and gradually increase the duration.

Hiking
·Take advantage of nature and hike, combining cardiovascular exercise with outdoor benefits.

Remember to start slowly, especially if you are new to exercising, and gradually increase intensity and duration. It's essential to consult with healthcare professionals before beginning any new exercise routine, especially if you have pre-existing health conditions. Consistency is vital, so find activities you enjoy to make fitness a sustainable part of your routine.

1.7 Managing Stress for Heart Health

Chronic stress can significantly impact heart health, increasing the risk of cardiovascular issues. Adopting effective stress management techniques is crucial for maintaining overall well-being. Here's a guide on managing stress to support heart health:

Exercise Regularly: Physical activity releases endorphins, the body's natural stress relievers. Choose activities you enjoy.

Practice Deep Breathing: Incorporate deep breathing exercises to activate the body's relaxation response. Focus on inhaling deeply through your nose, holding briefly, and exhaling slowly through your mouth.

Prioritize Sleep: Ensure adequate and quality sleep to rejuvenate the body and mind. Establish a consistent sleep routine and create a comfortable sleep environment.

Adopt Mindfulness Meditation: Practice mindfulness meditation to cultivate awareness of the present moment. Mindful breathing or guided meditation can help manage stress and promote relaxation.

Connect with Others: Maintain supportive social connections to share experiences and receive emotional support. Spending time with loved ones and friends can provide a sense of belonging and reduce stress.

Establish Boundaries: Set clear boundaries to manage work-related stress and prevent burnout. Learn to say no when necessary and prioritize self-care.

Engage in Relaxation Techniques: Explore techniques like progressive muscle relaxation or guided imagery. Find what works best for you to unwind and alleviate stress.

Limit Caffeine and Stimulant Intake: Monitor and moderate your consumption of caffeine and stimulants, which can contribute to increased anxiety and stress.

Practice Time Management: Break tasks into manageable steps to prevent feeling overwhelmed. Prioritize tasks and focus on one thing at a time.

Express Yourself Creatively: Engage in creative activities like art, music, or writing to express emotions and reduce stress. Finding outlets for self-expression can be therapeutic.

Laugh and Have Fun: Incorporate humor into your life by watching a funny movie, attending a comedy show, or spending time with people who make you laugh. Laughter triggers the release of endorphins, promoting a sense of well-being.

Identify Stress Triggers: Be aware of specific situations or events that trigger stress. Create effective methods for managing stressors and identifying solutions wherever feasible.

Seek Professional Support: If stress becomes overwhelming, consider seeking support from a mental health professional. Therapy or counseling can provide valuable tools and coping mechanisms.

Disconnect and Unplug: Take breaks from technology and social media to disconnect and reduce information overload. Establish periods for relaxation without constant digital stimulation.

Prioritizing stress management is a proactive step in safeguarding heart health.

Integrating these techniques into your daily regimen can establish a solid physical and mental wellness base. Seeking personalized guidance from healthcare experts is crucial, particularly if stress persists or hinders daily activities.

1.8 Monitoring Your Health: Regular Check-ups and Control

Regular medical check-ups and self-monitoring are vital in maintaining overall health, especially cardiovascular well-being. Here's an exploration of the significance of regular check-ups and some tips for self-monitoring key health indicators.

Significance of Regular Medical Check-ups:

1. Early Detection of Risk Factors:
·Regular check-ups allow healthcare professionals to assess risk factors for heart disease, such as high blood pressure, high cholesterol, and diabetes.
·Early detection enables timely intervention and lifestyle modifications to mitigate potential risks.

2. Blood Pressure Monitoring:
·Regular check-ups include monitoring blood pressure, a critical indicator of heart health.
·Controlling blood pressure is essential for preventing heart disease and related complications.

3. Cholesterol Levels Assessment:
·Routine check-ups involve measuring cholesterol levels, including LDL (bad cholesterol) and HDL (good cholesterol).
·Maintaining a healthy cholesterol profile is crucial for heart health.

4. Diabetes Screening:
·Regular testing for blood sugar levels helps identify diabetes or pre-diabetic conditions.
·Diabetes is a significant risk factor for heart disease.

5. Evaluation of Lifestyle Factors:
·Healthcare professionals assess lifestyle factors like diet, physical activity, smoking, and alcohol consumption during check-ups.
·Recommendations for healthy living are provided based on individual circumstances.

6. Monitoring Overall Cardiovascular Health:
·Comprehensive check-ups may include assessments of overall cardiovascular health, considering factors like BMI (Body Mass Index) and waist circumference.
·Holistic evaluations provide a more complete picture of heart health.

7. Preventive Screenings:
·Regular screenings for coronary artery disease and arrhythmias are essential for preventive care.
·Catching potential issues early allows for more effective management and intervention.

Tips for Self-Monitoring Health Indicators:

1. Blood Pressure Monitoring at Home:
·Invest in a home blood pressure monitor for regular self-checks.
·Keep a log of readings to share with healthcare professionals during check-ups.

2. Maintain a Health Journal:
·Record dietary habits, physical activity, and any symptoms experienced.
·A health journal can help identify patterns and areas for improvement.

3. Regular Physical Activity:
·Track your exercise routine and set realistic fitness goals.
·Regular physical activity contributes to cardiovascular health.

4. Healthy Eating Habits:
·Be mindful of your diet, focusing on nutrient-rich foods and portion control.
·Monitor your intake of saturated fats, trans fats, sodium, and added sugars.

5. Weight Management:
·Keep track of your weight and BMI regularly.
·Aim for a healthy weight range to reduce the risk of heart disease.

6. Monitor Cholesterol Levels:
·If advised by your healthcare provider, track your cholesterol levels at home.
·Make lifestyle adjustments based on your results.

7. Blood Sugar Monitoring:
·Individuals with or at risk of diabetes should monitor blood sugar levels regularly.
·Follow healthcare provider recommendations for self-monitoring.

8. Practice Stress Management Techniques:
·Monitor stress levels and practice stress management techniques such as deep breathing, meditation, or yoga.
·Identify triggers and take steps to address them.

9. Regular Sleep Patterns:
·Maintain consistent sleep patterns and monitor the quality of your sleep.
·Lack of sleep can contribute to cardiovascular issues.

10. Limit Smoking and Alcohol Consumption:
·Self-monitor and gradually reduce or eliminate smoking and excessive alcohol intake.
·Seek professional support if needed.

By blending regular medical examinations with proactive self-assessment, individuals can actively manage their heart health. Consistently monitoring essential markers and upholding a healthy lifestyle are vital to preventing heart disease and enhancing overall wellness. Seek personalized advice from healthcare professionals tailored to individual health circumstances.

1.9 Integrating Healthy Eating into Daily Life

Adopting a heart-healthy diet is a fundamental aspect of promoting cardiovascular well-being. Here's a guide on integrating healthy eating into your daily life:

·**Plan and Prep Meals:** Plan your weekly meals and prepare ingredients in advance. Having healthy options readily available reduces the temptation of less nutritious choices.

·**Snack Smartly:** Choose nutritious snacks like fresh fruit, raw veggies with hummus, or a handful of nuts. Avoid excessive consumption of processed snacks high in salt, sugar, and unhealthy fats.

·**Read Food Labels:** Familiarize yourself with food labels to make informed choices. Look for products with lower sodium, sugar, and saturated fat content.

·**Practice Mindful Eating:** Eat with awareness, savor each bite, and recognize hunger and fullness cues. Avoid distractions like screens during meals to enhance mindful eating.

·**Be Mindful of Emotional Eating:** Pay attention to emotional triggers that may lead to unhealthy eating habits. Find alternative ways to cope with stress, boredom, or other emotions.

·**Enjoy Social Eating Responsibly:** When dining out or socializing, make mindful choices by opting for healthier menu options. Share dishes to manage portion sizes and balance indulgences.

·**Treat Yourself Occasionally:** Allow yourself occasional treats to avoid feelings of deprivation. Moderation is essential, and indulging responsibly can be part of a balanced approach.

·**Explore Heart-Healthy Recipes:** Experiment with recipes prioritizing heart-healthy ingredients and cooking methods. Find joy in preparing and enjoying nutritious meals.

In wrapping up our exploration of caring for heart health through proper nutrition, we've delved into the essential components of a heart-healthy lifestyle. From understanding the fundamentals of heart-healthy eating to incorporating regular exercise, managing stress, and prioritizing check-ups, each step contributes to the well-being of your cardiovascular system.

In exploring how to take care of your heart health through proper nutrition, we delved into the essential components of a healthy lifestyle. From understanding the basics of a healthy diet to regular exercise, stress management, and prioritized screenings, every step contributes to cardiovascular well-being. Now, let's move on to a more detailed look at nutrition. We suggest you dive into the world of recipes for a healthy heart and enjoy delicious and nutritious food to live a long and healthy life.

Chapter 2: Breakfast Recipes

1 serving approximately:
9g protein 38g carbs
8g fat 50mg cholesterol
490mg sodium 440mg potassium

Whole Grain Pancakes

Ingredients:

- 1 cup whole wheat flour
- 1 tablespoon baking powder
- 1/4 teaspoon salt
- 1 cup low-fat milk
- 1 large egg
- 1 tablespoon maple syrup
- 1 ripe banana, mashed
- 1/4 cup chopped walnuts
- Cooking spray or oil for greasing the pan
- Optional toppings: Sliced bananas, additional chopped walnuts, Greek yogurt
- Orange fillets for decoration

Steps for Cooking:

1. Whisk the whole wheat flour, baking powder, and salt in a mixing bowl.
2. In a separate bowl, beat the egg and add milk, maple syrup, mashed banana, and chopped walnuts. Mix well to combine.
3. Pour the wet ingredients into the dry ingredients and stir until just combined. Do not overmix; a few lumps in the batter are okay.
4. Heat a non-stick skillet or griddle over medium heat and lightly grease with cooking spray or oil.
5. Pour about 1/4 cup of the pancake batter onto the skillet for each pancake. Cook until bubbles form on the surface and the edges look set, about 2-3 minutes.
6. Flip the pancakes and cook for another 1-2 minutes until golden brown and cooked through.
7. Arrange the cooked pancakes on serving plates. Decorate with orange fillets and any desired toppings, such as sliced bananas, chopped walnuts, or a dollop of Greek yogurt.

Servings 4
Prep time 10 Minutes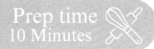
Cook time: 5 Minutes
Calories 280

Stuffed Peppers

Ingredient

- 2 large bell peppers, halved and seeds removed
- 1 can (15 oz) black beans, drained and rinsed
- 4 large eggs
- 1 cup diced tomatoes
- 1/2 cup diced red onion
- 1 jalapeño, finely chopped (seeds removed for less heat)
- 1 teaspoon ground cumin
- 1 teaspoon chili powder
- Salt and black pepper to taste
- Fresh cilantro and microgreens for garnish

Steps for Cooking:

1. Preheat the oven to 375°F (190°C). Place the halved bell peppers in a baking dish and set aside.
2. Mix black beans, diced tomatoes, red onion, jalapeño, ground cumin, chili powder, salt, and black pepper in a bowl.
3. Spoon the black bean mixture evenly into each bell pepper half, creating a well in the center.
4. Crack an egg into each well, and season the eggs with a pinch of salt and black pepper.
5. Bake in the oven for 20-25 minutes or until the egg whites are set, but the yolks are still slightly runny.

1 serving approximately:
14g protein 25g carbs
6g fat 180mg cholesterol
300mg sodium 600mg potassium

Servings	Prep time	Cook time:	Calories
4	15 Minutes	25 Minutes	320

---

1 serving approximately:
18g protein 30g carbs
15g fat 15mg cholesterol
70mg sodium 380mg potassium

Creamy Yogurt Delight

Ingredients:

- 1 cup Greek yogurt
- 1 tablespoon chia seeds
- 1 tablespoon ground flaxseed
- 1 tablespoon honey or maple syrup
- 1/2 cup mixed berries (such as blueberries, strawberries, raspberries)
- 2 tablespoons chopped walnuts or almonds
- Optional toppings: sliced bananas, shredded coconut, granola

Steps for Cooking:

1. Combine Greek yogurt, chia seeds, ground flaxseed, and honey or maple syrup in a small bowl.
2. Mix well until all ingredients are evenly distributed.
3. Layer the yogurt mixture with mixed berries and chopped nuts in serving glasses or bowls.
4. Repeat the layers until glasses or bowls are filled, ending with a layer of berries and nuts on top.
5. Garnish with optional toppings if desired.
6. Serve immediately or refrigerate until ready to eat.

Servings	Prep time	Cook time:	Calories
2	10 Minutes	0 Minutes	330

Green Smoothie Bowl

Ingredients

- 2 cups fresh spinach leaves
- 1 ripe banana, sliced and frozen
- 1/2 cup frozen pineapple chunks
- 1/2 avocado, peeled and pitted
- 1 tablespoon ground flaxseed
- 1/2 cup unsweetened almond milk or coconut water
- Toppings: sliced kiwi, sliced strawberries, granola, shredded coconut, chia seeds

Steps for Cooking:

1. Combine the fresh spinach leaves, frozen banana slices, pineapple chunks, avocado, ground flaxseed, and almond milk or coconut water in a blender.
2. Blend on high speed until smooth and creamy, adding more liquid to reach desired consistency.
3. Pour the green smoothie into bowls.
4. Top each bowl with sliced kiwi, strawberries, granola, shredded coconut, and chia seeds.

1 serving approximately:
7g protein 45g carbs
15g fat 0mg cholesterol
100mg sodium 860mg potassium

Servings	Prep time 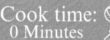	Cook time:	Calories
2	5 Minutes	0 Minutes	320

Broccoli and Cheese Quiche

Ingredients:

- 1 refrigerated pie crust (9 inches)
- 1 1/2 cups broccoli florets, blanched and chopped
- 1 cup shredded sharp cheddar cheese
- 4 large eggs
- 1 cup low-fat milk
- 1/2 teaspoon salt
- 1/4 teaspoon black pepper
- 1/4 teaspoon nutmeg (optional)

Steps for Cooking:

1. Preheat the oven to 375°F (190°C). Place the pie crust in a pie dish and crimp the edges.
2. Spread the blanched and chopped broccoli evenly over the pie crust. Sprinkle shredded cheddar cheese on top.
3. Whisk together the eggs, milk, salt, pepper, and nutmeg (if using).
4. Pour the egg mixture over the broccoli and cheese into the pie crust.
5. Bake in the oven for 35-40 minutes or until the center is set and the top is golden brown.

1 serving approximately:
18g protein 20g carbs
21g fat 210mg cholesterol
600mg sodium 320mg potassium

Servings	Prep time 	Cook time:	Calories
4	20 Minutes	35 Minutes	340

Apple Quinoa Porridge

Ingredient

- 1 cup quinoa, rinsed
- 2 cups water
- 1 cup unsweetened almond milk
- 2 medium apples, peeled, cored, and diced
- 1 teaspoon ground cinnamon
- 1 tablespoon maple syrup or honey (optional)
- 1/4 cup chopped hazelnuts (optional)
- Fresh apple slices, pomegranate and pumpkin seeds (optional)

Steps for Cooking:

1. In a medium saucepan, bring the water to a boil. Add the quinoa and reduce the heat to low. Cover and simmer for 15 minutes until quinoa is cooked and water is absorbed.
2. Stir in the almond milk, diced apples, ground cinnamon, and maple syrup or honey (if using). Cook for 5 minutes, stirring occasionally, until apples are softened and the mixture thickens.
3. Remove from heat and let the porridge sit for a few minutes to thicken further.
4. Serve the porridge garnished with chopped nuts, fresh apple slices, pomegranate, and pumpkin seeds.

1 serving approximately:
8g protein 55g carbs
7g fats 0mg cholesterol
90mg sodium 370mg potassium

Servings	Prep time 	Cook time:	Calories
4	5 Minutes	20 Minutes	320

1 serving approximately:
23g protein 28g carbs
20g fat 40mg cholesterol
520mg sodium 740mg potassium

Salmon Wrap

Ingredients:

- 2 whole wheat tortillas
- 6 oz cooked salmon fillet, flaked
- 1 cup fresh spinach leaves
- 1/2 avocado, sliced
- 1/4 cup diced tomatoes
- 2 tablespoons Greek yogurt
- 1 tablespoon chopped fresh dill (optional)
- Salt and pepper to taste

Steps for Cooking:

1. Warm the whole wheat tortillas in a skillet over medium heat for about 30 seconds on each side or until they are pliable.
2. Spread Greek yogurt evenly over each tortilla.
3. Divide the flaked salmon, fresh spinach leaves, sliced avocado, and diced tomatoes between the tortillas
4. Season with salt and pepper to taste, and sprinkle with chopped fresh dill if using.
5. Fold the sides of each tortilla over the filling, then roll tightly to form a wrap.

Servings	Prep time 	Cook time:	Calories
2	10 Minutes	10 Minutes	380

Sweet Potatoes and Eggs

Ingredients:

- 2 medium sweet potatoes, peeled and diced
- 2 tablespoons olive oil
- 2 cloves garlic, minced
- 1 teaspoon paprika
- Salt and pepper to taste
- 4 large eggs
- Chopped green onion for garnish (optional)

Steps for Cooking:

1. Preheat the oven to 400°F (200°C). Line a baking dish with parchment paper.
2. In a large bowl, toss the diced sweet potatoes with olive oil, minced garlic, paprika, salt, and pepper until evenly coated.
3. Spread the seasoned sweet potatoes in a single layer in the prepared baking dish. Bake in the preheated oven for 15 minutes.
4. After 15 minutes, remove the baking dish from the oven and use a spoon to make small wells in the sweet potatoes.
5. Crack one egg into each well, ensuring the egg stays within the well and doesn't overflow. Return the baking dish to the oven and continue baking for 8-10 minutes or until the eggs are set to your desired doneness.
6. Once done, remove the baked dish from the oven and let it cool slightly. Garnish with chopped green onions if desired.

1 serving approximately:
10g protein 28g carbs
18g fat 215mg cholesterol
320mg sodium 520mg potassium

Servings 2	Prep time 10 Minutes	Cook time: 25 Minutes	Calories 310

Mediterranean Omelette

1 serving approximately:
18g protein 7g carbs
9g fat 5mg cholesterol
420mg sodium 270mg potassium

Ingredients

- 6 large egg whites
- 1 tablespoon olive oil
- 1/4 cup diced red bell pepper
- 1/4 cup diced red onion
- 1/4 cup diced tomatoes
- 2 tablespoons chopped fresh spinach
- 2 tablespoons crumbled feta cheese
- Salt and pepper to taste
- Fresh chopped herbs for garnish (optional)

Steps for Cooking:

1. In a mixing bowl, whisk the egg whites until frothy. Season with salt and pepper to taste.
2. Heat olive oil in a non-stick skillet over medium heat. Add diced red bell pepper, red onion, and sauté until softened for 2-3 minutes.
3. Pour the whisked egg whites into the skillet, swirling to cover the bottom evenly.
4. Sprinkle diced tomatoes, chopped spinach, and crumbled feta cheese evenly over the egg whites.
5. Cook the omelet for 3-4 minutes until the edges are set and the bottom is golden brown. Carefully flip the omelet and cook for 2-3 minutes until cooked.

Servings  2	Prep time 10 Minutes	Cook time: 10 Minutes	Calories 180

Steel-cut oats

Ingredients:

- 1 cup steel-cut oats
- 3 cups water
- 1/4 teaspoon salt
- 2 tablespoons almond butter
- 2 ripe bananas, sliced
- Optional toppings: blueberry, walnut, chia seeds, honey or maple syrup, cinnamon

Steps for Cooking:

1. In a medium saucepan, bring the water to a boil. Stir in the steel-cut oats and salt.
2. Reduce the heat to low and simmer, uncovered, stirring occasionally, for about 20-25 minutes or until the oats are tender and have absorbed most of the water.
3. Remove the saucepan from the heat and stir in the almond butter until well combined.
4. Divide the cooked oats into serving bowls and top each with sliced bananas.
5. If desired, sprinkle with optional toppings such as blueberry, walnut, chia seeds, honey or maple syrup, and cinnamon.

1 serving approximately:
9g protein 55g carbs
11g fat 0mg cholesterol
75mg sodium 400mg potassium

Servings 	Prep time	Cook time:	Calories
4	5 Minutes	25 Minutes	350

---

1 serving approximately:
25g protein 40g carbs
10g fat 20mg cholesterol
300mg sodium 700mg potassium

Tuna and Mango Wrap

Ingredients:

- 2 whole grain tortillas
- 1 ripe mango, diced
- 1 medium carrot, cut into strips
- Handful of sprouts (e.g., alfalfa, broccoli sprouts)
- 1 cup shredded lettuce
- 1 can of tuna (5 oz), cubed
- 1/2 cup shredded blue cabbage
- Fresh lime wedges for garnish
- Hummus for spreading

Steps for Cooking:

1. Combine diced mango, carrot strips, sprouts, shredded lettuce, cubed tuna, and blue cabbage in a mixing bowl.
2. Heat a non-stick skillet. Spread a generous amount of hummus on one side of each whole-grain tortilla.
3. Divide the mango, carrot, sprout, tuna, and cabbage mixture equally between the two tortillas, placing it in the center in a horizontal line.
5. Fold the bottom edge of each tortilla up over the filling, then fold in the sides and roll tightly to form a wrap.
6. Place the wraps seam-side down in the skillet and cook for 2-3 minutes until golden brown and crispy.

Servings	Prep time	Cook time:	Calories
2	15 Minutes	5 Minutes	340

Turkey Sausage Skillet

Ingredients:

- 8 oz turkey sausage, sliced
- 1 small onion, diced
- 1 bell pepper, diced
- 2 cups sliced mushrooms
- 2 cups fresh spinach leaves
- 4 large eggs
- Salt and pepper to taste
- Optional toppings: chopped fresh herbs, feta cheese

Steps for Cooking:

1. Add the sliced turkey sausage to a large, non-stick skillet over medium heat. Cook until browned, about 5 minutes, stirring occasionally to prevent sticking.
2. Add diced onion and bell pepper to the skillet. Sauté until vegetables are softened, about 3-4 minutes.
3. Stir in sliced mushrooms and cook for 3-4 minutes until mushrooms are tender.
4. Add fresh spinach leaves to the skillet and cook until wilted about 2 minutes.
5. Create four wells in the vegetable mixture and crack an egg into each well. Season the eggs with salt and pepper.
6. Cover the skillet and cook until the eggs are set to your desired doneness, about 5 minutes for runny yolks or longer for firmer yolks. Once eggs are cooked, sprinkle them with chopped fresh herbs and feta cheese.

1 serving approximately:
22g protein 12g carbs
18g fat 230mg cholesterol
620mg sodium 540mg potassium

Servings
4

Prep time
10 Minutes

Cook time:
15 Minutes

Calories
320

Salmon Poke Bowl

1 serving approximately:
31g protein 37g carbs
18g fat 70mg cholesterol
550mg sodium 800mg potassium

Ingredients:

- 1 pound fresh salmon fillet
- 2 cups cooked brown rice
- 1 cup Chuka salad
- 1/2 cup sliced radishes
- 1/2 cup sliced cucumbers
- 1 ripe avocado, sliced
- 2 tablespoons sesame seeds
- 2 tablespoons chopped green onions for garnish
- 1/4 cup low-sodium soy sauce
- 1 tablespoon sesame oil
- 1 tablespoon rice vinegar
- 1 teaspoon fresh ginger
- 1teaspoon honey
- 1 clove garlic, minced

Steps for Cooking:

1. In a bowl, combine the marinade ingredients: low-sodium soy sauce, sesame oil, rice vinegar, grated fresh ginger, honey, and minced garlic. Whisk well.
2. Place the cubed salmon in a shallow dish and pour the marinade. Toss gently to coat the salmon pieces evenly. Cover the dish and refrigerate for at least 15 minutes to marinate.
3. Meanwhile, prepare the other ingredients. Cook the brown rice according to package instructions if not already cooked.
4. Arrange the cooked brown rice to be served in bowls. Top the rice with marinated salmon cubes. Add sliced radishes, cucumbers, avocado, and Chuka salad to the rice. Sprinkle sesame seeds and chopped green onions over the bowl before serving.

Servings
4

Prep time
20 Minutes

Cook time:
0 Minutes

Calories
420

Overnight Oats

Ingredients:

- 1 cup rolled oats
- 1 1/2 cups unsweetened almond milk
- 2 tablespoons chia seeds
- 1/4 cup sliced almonds
- 2 tablespoons honey or maple syrup (optional)
- Fresh berries or sliced fruits for topping (optional)

Steps for Cooking:

1. Combine rolled oats, almond milk, chia seeds, and sliced almonds in a mixing bowl. If desired, add honey or maple syrup for sweetness.
2. Stir the mixture until well combined, ensuring that the oats and chia seeds are evenly distributed.
3. Divide the mixture into two serving jars or containers with lids.
4. Cover the jars or containers and refrigerate them overnight or for at least 6 hours to allow the oats and chia seeds to absorb the liquid and soften. Before serving, stir the overnight oats. Top with fresh berries or sliced fruits.

1 serving approximately:
10g protein 45g carbs
15g fat 0mg cholesterol
150mg sodium 300mg potassium

 Servings 2    Prep time 10 Minutes   Cook time: 0 Minutes   Calories 350

Salmon Quesadilla

1 serving approximately:
33 protein 30g carbs
20g fat 290mg cholesterol
570mg sodium 620mg potassium

Ingredients:

- 2 large whole wheat tortillas
- 4 large eggs
- 4 oz cooked salmon fillet, flaked
- 1 medium tomato, thinly sliced
- 1/2 cup shredded low-fat cheese
- 1 tablespoon olive oil
- Salt and pepper to taste
- Chopped dill and micro greens for garnish

Steps for Cooking:

1. In a bowl, beat the eggs and season with salt and pepper.
2. Heat olive oil in a non-stick skillet over medium heat. Pour in the beaten eggs and cook, stirring occasionally, until they are set but still moist. Remove the omelet from the skillet and set aside.
3. Place one whole wheat tortilla in the skillet. Arrange half of the omelet, flaked salmon, sliced tomatoes, and shredded cheese evenly over the tortilla.
4. Top with the second tortilla and press down gently with a spatula.
5. Cook the quesadilla for 2-3 minutes on each side until the tortilla is golden brown and the cheese is melted. Remove the quesadilla from the skillet and cut it into wedges.

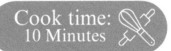 Servings 2   Prep time 10 Minutes   Cook time: 10 Minutes   Calories 430

Blueberry Smoothie Bowl

Ingredients:

- 1 cup frozen blueberries
- 1 ripe banana
- 1/2 cup plain Greek yogurt
- 2 tablespoons natural peanut butter
- 1/2 cup almond milk (unsweetened)
- 1/4 cup whole wheat unsweetened cereal
- Fresh berries (blueberries, strawberries) for garnish
- Chopped nuts (almonds, walnuts) for garnish (optional)
- Honey or maple syrup for drizzling (optional)

Steps for Cooking:

1. Combine the frozen blueberries, ripe banana, Greek yogurt, peanut butter, and almond milk in a blender. Blend until smooth and creamy.
2. Pour the smoothie mixture into serving bowls.
3. Sprinkle the whole wheat unsweetened cereal evenly over the smoothie bowls.
4. Garnish each bowl with fresh blueberries, sliced strawberries, chopped nuts (if using), and a drizzle of honey or maple syrup if desired.

1 serving approximately:
14 protein 40g carbs
14g fat 10mg cholesterol
120mg sodium 550mg potassium

Servings	Prep time 	Cook time:	Calories
2	10 Minutes	10 Minutes	320

Banana Casserole

1 serving approximately:
14 protein 32g carbs
7g fat 135mg cholesterol
220mg sodium 320mg potassium

Ingredients:

- 1 cup low-fat cottage cheese
- 2 eggs, beaten
- 1/4 cup honey or maple syrup
- 1/2 teaspoon vanilla extract
- 1/4 cup almond flour
- 1 ripe banana, mashed
- 1/4 teaspoon cinnamon
- 1/8 teaspoon salt
- Fresh mint leaves for garnish
- Sliced banana and blueberries for garnish

Steps for Cooking:

1. Preheat your oven to 350°F (175°C). Grease a baking dish with cooking spray or oil.
2. Combine the cottage cheese, beaten eggs, honey or maple syrup, mashed banana, almond flour, vanilla extract, cinnamon, and salt in a mixing bowl. Mix well.
3. Spread the cottage cheese mixture evenly into the greased baking dish.
4. Lightly sprinkle some cinnamon on the cottage cheese mixture for added flavor.
5. Bake in the oven for 30 minutes or until the top is golden brown.
6. Remove from the oven and allow it to cool slightly before serving.
7. Garnish with fresh mint leaves, sliced banana, and blueberries when serving.

Servings	Prep time 	Cook time: 	Calories
4	15 Minutes	30 Minutes	240

Veggie Muffins

Ingredients

- 6 large eggs
- 1/2 cup diced bell peppers (any color)
- 1/2 cup diced tomatoes
- 1/2 cup chopped spinach
- 1/4 cup diced onions
- 1/4 cup shredded cheddar cheese
- Salt and pepper to taste
- Cooking spray
- 1/2 cup plain Greek yogurt

Steps for Cooking:

1. Preheat your oven to 350°F (175°C) and lightly grease a muffin tin with cooking spray
2. Whisk together the eggs, diced bell peppers, tomatoes, spinach, onions, shredded cheddar cheese, salt, and pepper in a mixing bowl.
3. Pour the egg mixture evenly into the prepared muffin tin, filling each cup about 3/4 full.
4. Bake in the oven for about 18-20 minutes or until the frittata muffins are set and lightly golden on top.
5. Remove the muffin tin from the oven and let the frittata muffins cool slightly.
6. Serve Muffins with a dollop of plain Greek yogurt on top.

1 serving approximately:
15g protein 10g carbs
15g fat 280mg cholesterol
350mg sodium 450mg potassium

Servings 	Prep time	Cook time:	Calories
4	15 Minutes	20 Minutes	250

Oatmeal with Chicken

1 serving approximately:
30 protein 35g carbs
12g fat 70mg cholesterol
450mg sodium 600mg potassium

Ingredients:

- 1 cup steel-cut oats
- 2 cups water
- 1/2 teaspoon salt
- 1 pound chicken breasts, grilled and sliced
- 1 cup diced cucumber
- 1 cup diced red pepper
- 1 cup shredded lettuce
- 1/2 cup micro greens
- 2 tablespoons chopped fresh dill
- 2 tablespoons sesame seeds
- 3 tablespoons olive oil
- 1 tablespoon lemon juice
- 1 teaspoon honey

Steps for Cooking:

1. In a saucepan, bring the water and salt to a boil. Stir in the steel-cut oats and reduce heat to low. Cook uncovered, stirring occasionally for 15-20 minutes or until oats are tender and reach your desired consistency.
2. While the oats are cooking, prepare the grilled chicken. Season the chicken breasts with salt and pepper, then grill until cooked. Slice the grilled chicken into thin strips.
3. Whisk together the olive oil, lemon juice, honey, salt, and pepper in a small bowl to make the dressing.
4. In serving bowls, divide the cooked oatmeal evenly. Top the oatmeal with grilled chicken slices, diced cucumber, diced red pepper, shredded lettuce, and micro greens. Drizzle the dressing over the oatmeal and chicken.

Servings	Prep time	Cook time:	Calories
4	15 Minutes	20 Minutes	380

1 serving approximately:
10g protein 50g carbs
20g fat 0mg cholesterol
300mg sodium 800mg potassium

Buddha Bowl with Quinoa

Ingredients

- 1 cup quinoa
- 1 can chickpeas, drained and rinsed
- 1 cucumber, diced
- 1 cup cherry tomatoes, halved
- 2 cups spinach leaves
- 4 radishes, thinly sliced
- 1 cup shredded carrots
- 2 avocados, halved
- 2 tablespoons sesame seeds
- Salt and pepper to taste
- Olive oil for drizzling

Steps for Cooking:

1. Cook the quinoa according to the package instructions. Once cooked, fluff with a fork and set aside to cool slightly.
2. Pile-cooked quinoa, chickpeas, diced cucumber, halved cherry tomatoes, spinach leaves, sliced radishes, and shredded carrots in a serving bowl.
3. Halve the avocados and remove the pit. Place one avocado half in the middle of each serving bowl.
4. Drizzle olive oil over the ingredients in the bowl and season with salt and pepper to taste.
5. Sprinkle sesame seeds over each avocado half and the bowl mixture.

Servings 4

Prep time 20 Minutes

Cook time: 15 Minutes

Calories 400

Grilled Eggplant

Ingredients:

- 2 large eggplants, sliced into 1/2-inch rounds
- 2 tablespoons olive oil
- Salt and pepper to taste
- 1/2 cup pomegranate seeds
- Fresh parsley, chopped, for garnish

Steps for Cooking:

1. Preheat a grill or grill pan over medium-high heat.
2. Brush both sides of the eggplant slices with olive oil and season with salt and pepper.
3. Grill the eggplant slices for 5-7 minutes per side until they are tender and have grill marks.
4. Remove the grilled eggplant slices from the grill and arrange them on a serving platter.
5. Sprinkle the pomegranate seeds over the grilled eggplant slices.
6. Garnish with chopped fresh parsley or other favorite greens before serving

1 serving approximately:
2g protein 10g carbs
8g fat 0mg cholesterol
10mg sodium 300mg potassium

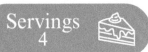 **Servings** 4
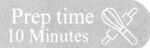 **Prep time** 10 Minutes
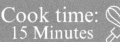 **Cook time:** 15 Minutes
 Calories 120

---

1 serving approximately:
3g protein 8g carbs
7g fat 0mg cholesterol
150mg sodium 300mg potassium

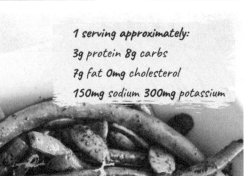

Green Bean Almondine

Ingredients:

- 1 lb fresh green beans, trimmed
- 2 tablespoons olive oil
- 2 tablespoons sliced almonds
- 2 cloves garlic, minced
- 1 tablespoon lemon juice
- Salt and pepper to taste
- Lemon zest for garnish (optional)

Steps for Cooking:

1. Bring a pot of salted water to a boil. Add the green beans and cook for about 4-5 minutes until they are tender-crisp. Drain the beans and set aside.
2. In a large skillet, heat olive oil over medium heat. Add the sliced almonds and toast them until golden brown, stirring frequently for 2-3 minutes.
3. Add the minced garlic to the skillet and sauté for another minute until fragrant. Add the cooked green beans to the skillet, along with lemon juice, salt, and pepper. Toss everything together to coat the beans evenly with the almond and garlic mixture.
4. Cook for 2-3 minutes, stirring occasionally, until the beans are heated and well coated with the flavors.

 **Servings** 4
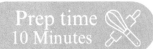 **Prep time** 10 Minutes
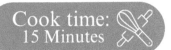 **Cook time:** 15 Minutes
 Calories 100

Stewed Bulgur

Ingredients:

- 1 cup bulgur wheat
- 2 cups vegetable broth
- 1 tablespoon olive oil
- 1 onion, chopped
- 2 garlic cloves, minced
- 1 bell pepper, diced
- 1 zucchini, diced
- 1 carrot, diced
- 1 can (14 oz) diced tomatoes, undrained
- 1 teaspoon dried oregano
- Salt and pepper to taste
- Fresh parsley for garnish

Steps for Cooking:

1. In a medium saucepan, bring the vegetable broth to a boil. Add the bulgur wheat, cover, and simmer for about 15 minutes or until the bulgur is tender and has absorbed the liquid. Remove from heat and set aside.
2. In a large skillet, heat olive oil over medium heat. Add chopped onion and garlic, and sauté until translucent and fragrant. Add diced bell pepper, zucchini, and carrot to the skillet. Cook for about 5-7 minutes until the vegetables are slightly tender.
3. Stir in the canned diced tomatoes (including the juice) and dried oregano. Season with salt and pepper to taste. Add the cooked bulgur to the skillet with the vegetables. Stir well to combine all the ingredients. Cook for 5-7 minutes, allowing the flavors to meld together.

1 serving approximately:
8g protein 50g carbs
7g fat 0mg cholesterol
400mg sodium 550mg potassium

Servings	Prep time	Cook time:	Calories
4	15 Minutes	25 Minutes	300

Cauliflower Rice

1 serving approximately:
3g protein 7g carbs
5g fat 0mg cholesterol
150mg sodium 400mg potassium

Ingredients

- 1 large head cauliflower, grated into rice-like pieces
- 2 tablespoons olive oil
- 2 cloves garlic, minced
- 1 teaspoon dried thyme
- 1 teaspoon dried oregano
- Salt and pepper to taste
- Juice of 1 lemon
- Fresh parsley, chopped, for garnish

Steps for Cooking:

1. Heat olive oil in a large skillet over medium heat. Add minced garlic and sauté until fragrant.
2. Add the grated cauliflower rice to the skillet. Season with dried thyme, dried oregano, salt, and pepper.
3. Stir well to combine and cook for 5-7 minutes until the cauliflower rice is tender but not mushy.
4. Remove the skillet from heat and drizzle the lemon juice over the cauliflower rice. Toss to coat evenly.
5. Transfer the cauliflower rice to a serving bowl and garnish with chopped fresh parsley before serving.

Servings	Prep time	Cook time:	Calories
4	10 Minutes	10 Minutes	80

Pesto Pasta

Ingredients:

- 8 ounces whole wheat pasta
- 1/2 cup basil pesto (store-bought or homemade)
- 1 pint cherry tomatoes, halved
- 1 cup fresh mozzarella balls, halved
- 2 tablespoons olive oil
- Salt and pepper to taste
- Fresh basil leaves for garnish

1 serving approximately:
15g protein 45g carbs
18g fat 20mg cholesterol
300mg sodium 400mg potassium

Steps for Cooking:

1. Cook the whole wheat pasta according to the package instruction until al dente. Drain and set aside.
2. In a large skillet, heat the olive oil over medium heat. Add the cherry tomatoes and sauté until they soften, about 3-4 minutes.
3. Add the cooked pasta to the skillet with the cherry tomatoes. Stir in the basil pesto and toss everything together until the pasta is well-coated.
4. Add the fresh mozzarella balls to the skillet and gently stir to combine. Cook for another 2-3 minutes until the mozzarella melts slightly.
5. Season with salt and pepper to taste. Remove from heat.

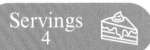 **Servings** 4

 **Prep time** 10 Minutes

 **Cook time:** 12 Minutes

 Calories 400

---

1 serving approximately:
4g protein 40g carbs
12g fat 0mg cholesterol
250mg sodium 800mg potassium

Greek Roasted Potatoes

Ingredients:

- 2 lbs (about 4 medium-sized) russet potatoes, washed and cut into wedges
- 3 tablespoons olive oil
- 2 tablespoons fresh lemon juice
- 2 teaspoons dried oregano
- 1 teaspoon garlic powder
- Salt and black pepper to taste
- Fresh parsley or dill for garnish (optional)

Steps for Cooking:

1. Preheat your oven to 400°F (200°C) and line a baking sheet with parchment paper.
2. Combine the olive oil, lemon juice, dried oregano, garlic powder, salt, and black pepper in a large bowl. Whisk until well combined.
3. Add the potato wedges to the bowl with the seasoning mixture. Toss the potatoes until they are evenly coated.
4. Arrange the seasoned potato wedges on the prepared baking sheet in a single layer.
5. Roast the potatoes in the oven for about 35-40 minutes, or until golden brown and crispy, flipping them halfway through cooking for even browning.
6. Once roasted, remove the potatoes from the oven and transfer them to a serving dish.

 **Servings** 4

Prep time 15 Minutes

Cook time: 40 Minutes

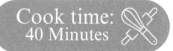 **Calories** 280

Stuffed Zucchini Boats

Ingredients:

- 2 large zucchinis
- 1 tablespoon olive oil
- 1 onion, chopped
- 2 cloves garlic, minced
- 1 bell pepper, diced
- 1 eggplant, diced
- 1 zucchini, diced
- 1 cup cherry tomatoes, halved
- 2 tablespoons tomato paste
- 1 teaspoon dried thyme
- 1 teaspoon dried oregano
- Salt and pepper to taste
- 1/4 cup grated Parmesan cheese

Steps for Cooking:

1. Preheat your oven to 375°F (190°C). Line a baking dish with parchment paper.
2. Cut the zucchinis in half lengthwise and scoop out the flesh to create "boats." Chop the scooped-out zucchini flesh and set aside.
3. Heat olive oil in a large skillet over medium heat. Add chopped onion and minced garlic, sautéing until the onion is translucent, about 3-4 minutes. Add diced bell pepper, eggplant, zucchini, cherry tomatoes, and the reserved chopped zucchini flesh to the skillet.

Cook for about 5-6 minutes until the vegetables are tender.
4. Stir in tomato paste, dried thyme, oregano, salt, and pepper. Cook for an additional 2 minutes. Fill each zucchini boat with the ratatouille mixture and place them in the prepared baking dish. Sprinkle-grated Parmesan cheese (if using) over the stuffed zucchini boats.
5. Cover the baking dish with foil and bake in the oven for 20 minutes. Remove the foil and bake for 10-15 minutes until the zucchini boats are tender and the cheese is melted.

1 serving approximately:
6g protein 15g carbs
10g fat 5mg cholesterol
300mg sodium 700mg potassium

 Servings 4
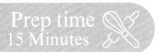 Prep time 15 Minutes
 Cook time: 35 Minutes
 Calories 200

Spicy Sweet Potato

1 serving approximately:
2g protein 28g carbs
7g fat 0mg cholesterol
190mg sodium 550mg potassium

Ingredients:

- 2 large sweet potatoes, peeled and sliced
- 2 tablespoons olive oil
- 1 teaspoon paprika
- 1/2 teaspoon cayenne pepper
- 1/2 teaspoon garlic powder
- Salt and black pepper to taste
- Fresh cilantro or parsley for garnish (optional)

Steps for Cooking:

1. Preheat the oven to 400°F (200°C) and line a baking sheet with parchment paper.
2. Mix olive oil, paprika, cayenne pepper, garlic powder, salt, and black pepper in a bowl.
3. Add the sweet potato slices to the bowl and toss until evenly coated with the spice mixture.
4. Arrange the seasoned sweet potato slices in a single layer on the prepared baking sheet.
5. Bake in the preheated oven for about 20-25 minutes or until the sweet potato slices are tender and golden brown, flipping them halfway through for even cooking.
6. Once cooked, remove from the oven and let cool slightly.

 Servings 4
  Prep time 10 Minutes
 Cook time: 25 Minutes
 Calories 170

Vegetable Ratatouille

Ingredients

- 1 medium eggplant, diced
- 2 small zucchinis, sliced
- 2 large tomatoes, diced
- 1 onion, chopped
- 2 garlic cloves, minced
- 2 tablespoons olive oil
- 1 teaspoon dried oregano
- 1 teaspoon dried thyme
- Salt and black pepper to taste
- Fresh basil leaves for garnish

Steps for Cooking:

1. Preheat the oven to 400°F (200°C).
2. Combine the diced eggplant, sliced zucchini, tomatoes, chopped onion, and minced garlic in a large baking dish.
3. Drizzle olive oil over the vegetables and sprinkle with dried oregano, thyme, salt, and black pepper. Toss to coat evenly.
4. Cover the baking dish with foil and bake in the oven for 20 minutes.
5. Remove the foil and continue baking for 10 minutes or until the vegetables are tender and slightly caramelized.
6. Remove from the oven and let it cool slightly before serving.
7. Garnish with fresh basil leaves for added flavor and aroma.

1 serving approximately:
2g protein 15g carbs
7g fat 0mg cholesterol
180mg sodium 600mg potassium

 Servings 4
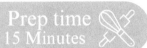 Prep time 15 Minutes
 Cook time: 30 Minutes
 Calories 120

1 serving approximately:
5g protein 10g carbs
7g fat 0mg cholesterol
200mg sodium 600mg potassium

Roasted Cauliflower

Ingredients

- 1 large head of cauliflower
- 2 tablespoons olive oil
- 2 teaspoons smoked paprika
- 1 teaspoon garlic powder
- 1 teaspoon onion powder
- 1/2 teaspoon ground cumin
- Salt and black pepper to taste
- Fresh parsley for garnish (optional)

Steps for Cooking:

1. Preheat the oven to 400°F (200°C).
2. Remove any green leaves from the cauliflower and trim the stem so it sits flat in a baking dish.
3. In a small bowl, mix the olive oil, smoked paprika, garlic powder, onion powder, ground cumin, salt, and black pepper to form a paste.
4. Brush the cauliflower with the spice paste and coat it evenly. Place the cauliflower in a baking dish lined with parchment paper.
5. Roast the cauliflower in the oven for about 40 minutes or until tender and golden brown outside. Remove the roasted cauliflower from the oven and let it cool slightly before serving. Garnish with fresh parsley if desired.

Servings 4
Prep time 10 Minutes
 Cook time: 40 Minutes
 Calories 120

Lemon Herb Couscous

Ingredients

- 1 cup whole wheat couscous
- 1 1/4 cups low-sodium vegetable broth
- 1 tablespoon olive oil
- 1 tablespoon lemon zest
- 2 tablespoons fresh lemon juice
- 2 tablespoons chopped fresh parsley
- 1/4 teaspoon garlic powder
- Salt and pepper to taste
- Lemon slices and additional chopped parsley for serving

Steps for Cooking:

1. In a medium saucepan, bring the low-sodium vegetable broth to a boil.
2. Stir in the whole wheat couscous, cover the saucepan with a lid, and remove it from heat. Let it sit covered for about 5 minutes to allow the couscous to absorb the broth.
3. After 5 minutes, fluff the couscous with a fork to separate the grains.
4. Whisk together the olive oil, lemon zest, fresh lemon juice, chopped parsley, garlic powder, salt, and pepper in a small bowl.
5. Pour the lemon herb dressing over the cooked couscous and toss gently to coat evenly.
6. Transfer the lemon herb couscous to a serving bowl. Garnish with lemon slices and additional chopped parsley before serving.

1 serving approximately:
5g protein 30g carbs
5g fat 0mg cholesterol
150mg sodium 200mg potassium

 Servings 4    **Prep time** 10 Minutes   **Cook time:** 10 Minutes   **Calories** 180

Stuffed Tomatoes

1 serving approximately:
6g protein 25g carbs
7g fat 0mg cholesterol
150mg sodium 450mg potassium

Ingredients:

- 4 large tomatoes
- 1 cup cooked quinoa
- 1 cup fresh spinach, chopped
- 1/2 cup red bell pepper, diced
- 1/4 cup red onion, chopped
- 2 cloves garlic, minced
- 1 tablespoon olive oil
- 1 teaspoon dried oregano
- 1/2 teaspoon paprika
- Salt and pepper to taste
- 1/4 cup grated Parmesan cheese (optional)

Steps for Cooking:

1. Preheat your oven to 375°F (190°C). Cut the tops off the tomatoes and scoop the seeds and pulp using a spoon to create tomato cups.
2. Combine cooked quinoa, chopped spinach, diced red bell pepper, chopped red onion, minced garlic, olive oil, dried oregano, paprika, salt, and pepper in a large mixing bowl. Mix well to combine all ingredients.
3. Stuff each tomato with the quinoa and spinach mixture, pressing gently to fill the tomatoes evenly.
4. Place the stuffed tomatoes in a baking dish or on a baking sheet lined with parchment paper. If desired, sprinkle grated Parmesan cheese on top of each stuffed tomato. Bake in the preheated oven for about 20-25 minutes or until the tomatoes are tender and the filling is heated.

 Servings 4    **Prep time** 15 Minutes    **Cook time:** 25 Minutes   **Calories** 180

Grilled Vegetable Platter

Ingredients:

- 1 medium eggplant, sliced into rounds
- 2 zucchinis, sliced lengthwise
- 1 red bell pepper, seeded and quartered
- 1 yellow bell pepper, seeded and quartered
- 1 red onion, sliced into rounds
- 8 button mushrooms, cleaned and halved
- 8 cherry tomatoes
- 1 cup string beans, trimmed
- 2 tablespoons olive oil
- 2 tablespoons balsamic vinegar
- Fresh basil leaves for garnish

Steps for Cooking:

1. Preheat the grill to medium-high heat. Brush the eggplant, zucchini, bell pepper quarters, onion rounds, mushrooms, cherry tomatoes, and string beans with olive oil. Season with salt and pepper.
2. Place the vegetables on the preheated grill and cook for about 5-minutes per side until they are tender and have grill marks.
3. Meanwhile, in a small saucepan, heat the balsamic vinegar over medium heat until it reduces and thickens slightly, about 3-5 minutes.
4. Arrange the grilled vegetables on a platter, drizzle the balsamic glaze, and garnish with fresh basil leaves.

1 serving approximately:
5g protein 20g carbs
12g fat 0mg cholesterol
320mg sodium 720mg potassium

Servings 4	Prep time 15 Minutes	Cook time: 15 Minutes	Calories 190

1 serving approximately:
7g protein 35g carbs
6g fat 0mg cholesterol
450mg sodium 350mg potassium

Quinoa Pilaf

Ingredients:

- 1 cup quinoa, rinsed
- 2 cups vegetable broth
- 1 tablespoon olive oil
- 1 small onion, chopped
- 2 cloves garlic, minced
- 1 medium carrot, diced
- 1 red bell pepper, diced
- 1 cup frozen peas
- 1 teaspoon ground cumin
- Salt and black pepper to taste
- Fresh parsley for garnish

Steps for Cooking:

1. Combine the quinoa and vegetable broth in a medium saucepan. Bring to a boil, then reduce heat, cover, and simmer for about 15 minutes or until the quinoa is tender and the liquid is absorbed.
2. In a large skillet, heat olive oil over medium heat. Add the chopped onion and minced garlic, and sauté until softened and fragrant.
3. Add the diced carrot and red bell pepper to the skillet. Cook for about 5 minutes until the vegetables are slightly tender.
4. Stir in the cooked quinoa, frozen peas, ground cumin, salt, and black pepper. Cook for 5 minutes, stirring occasionally, until the peas are heated.

Servings 4	Prep time 10 Minutes	Cook time: 20 Minutes	Calories 220

1 serving approximately:
14g protein 15g carbs
22g fat 35mg cholesterol
530mg sodium 330mg potassium

Grilled Halloumi and Rocket Salad

Ingredients:

- 1 pack (about 8 oz) halloumi cheese, sliced
- 4 cups fresh rocket (arugula) leaves
- 1 large orange, peeled and segmented
- 1 cup cherry tomatoes, halved
- 1/2 cup pomegranate arils
- 1/4 cup thinly sliced red onion
- 1/4 cup extra virgin olive oil
- 2 tablespoons balsamic vinegar
- Salt and black pepper to taste

Steps for Cooking:

1. Preheat a grill or grill pan over medium-high heat.
2. Whisk together the extra virgin olive oil, balsamic vinegar, salt, and black pepper in a small bowl to make the dressing.
3. Brush the halloumi cheese slices lightly with some dressing on both sides.
4. Grill the halloumi slices for 2-3 minutes per side or until grill marks appear and the cheese is heated through.
5. Combine the rocket leaves, orange segments, pomegranate arils, sliced red onion, and halved cherry tomatoes in a large mixing bowl.
6. Drizzle the remaining dressing over the salad ingredients and toss gently to coat everything evenly.
7. Divide the dressed salad onto serving plates and top each with grilled halloumi slices.

Servings	Prep time	Cook time:	Calories
4	15 Minutes	10 Minutes	310

Chicken Vegetable Bowl

Ingredients:

- 1 lb boneless, skinless chicken breasts (about 2 breasts)
- 1 cup quinoa, cooked
- 1 can (15 oz) chickpeas, drained and rinsed
- 2 cups fresh spinach leaves
- 1 avocado, sliced
- 1 cup Brussels sprouts, halved
- 1 red bell pepper, sliced
- 2 tablespoons olive oil
- Salt and pepper to taste
- Fresh cilantro and black sesame seeds for garnish

Steps for Cooking:

1. Preheat the grill to medium-high heat
2. Season the chicken breasts with salt and pepper, then grill for 6-8 minutes per side or until fully cooked. Remove from the grill and let rest before slicing
3. Place the halved Brussels sprouts in a large mixing bowl.
4. Heat 1 tablespoon of olive oil over medium heat in a separate skillet. Add the chickpeas and cooked quinoa. Sauté for about 3-4 minutes until heated through. Add the chickpeas and quinoa mixture to the bowl with Brussels sprouts. Toss the raw Brussels sprouts, chickpeas, and quinoa until well combined.
5. To assemble the bowls, divide the spinach leaves among serving bowls. Top with the grilled chicken slices, raw Brussels sprouts, and chickpea-quinoa mixture. Garnish each bowl with sliced avocado, grilled red pepper slices, fresh cilantro, and black sesame seeds.

1 serving approximately:
30g protein 30g carbs
20g fat 60mg cholesterol
350mg sodium 900mg potassium

Servings 4	Prep time 20 Minutes	Cook time: 20 Minutes	Calories 430

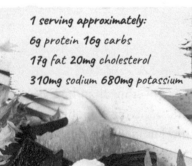
1 serving approximately:
6g protein 16g carbs
17g fat 20mg cholesterol
310mg sodium 680mg potassium

Beet Salad with Orange

Ingredients:

- 2 medium-sized beets, cooked and cubed
- 1 large orange, peeled and segmented
- 1/2 cup crumbled feta cheese
- 1 cup fresh arugula
- 1/4 cup pine nuts
- Fresh cilantro or parsley

For the Dressing:
- 3 tablespoons olive oil
- 2 tablespoons balsamic vinegar
- 1 teaspoon honey

Steps for Cooking:

1. Combine the cubed beets, orange segments, crumbled feta cheese, fresh arugula, and pine nuts in a large salad bowl.
2. Whisk together the olive oil, balsamic vinegar, honey, salt, and pepper in a small bowl to make the dressing.
3. Pour the dressing over the salad ingredients and gently toss to coat everything evenly.
4. Garnish with fresh cilantro or parsley leaves before serving.

Servings 4	Prep time 20 Minutes	Cook time: 0 Minutes	Calories 230

Chicken and Mango Salad

Ingredients:

- 2 boneless, skinless chicken breasts
- 2 tablespoons olive oil
- 4 cups lettuce leaves
- 1 cup cherry tomatoes, halved
- 1 ripe avocado, diced
- 1 mango, peeled and cubed
- 1/2 red onion, thinly sliced
- Fresh cilantro leaves, chopped
- 1 yellow pepper, diced
- Lime wedges (for serving)
- 1 mango, peeled and diced
- 1/4 cup chopped red onion
- 1/4 cup chopped fresh cilantro
- 1 small jalapeno pepper, seeded and minced
- Juice of 1 lime

Steps for Cooking:

1. Preheat the grill or grill pan over medium-high heat.
2. Rub the chicken breasts with olive oil and season with salt and pepper.
3. Grill the chicken for 6-7 minutes per side or until cooked through. Remove from heat and let it rest for a few minutes before slicing.
4. Combine the lettuce leaves, cherry tomatoes, avocado, cubed mango, sliced red onion, chopped cilantro, and diced yellow pepper in a large bowl.
5. To make the mango salsa, mix the diced mango, red onion, cilantro, jalapeno pepper, lime juice, and salt in a separate bowl.
6. Add the sliced grilled chicken to the salad bowl and toss everything together gently.
7. Serve salad on individual plates, garnished with lime wedges and a dollop of mango salsa on top.

1 serving approximately:
24g protein 22g carbs
16g fat 60mg cholesterol
350mg sodium 900mg potassium

Servings 4	Prep time 15 Minutes	Cook time: 15 Minutes	Calories 320

Quinoa Salad

1 serving approximately:
5g protein 32g carbs
8g fat 0mg cholesterol
200mg sodium 270mg potassium

Ingredients:

- 1 cup quinoa
- 2 cups water
- 1 cup tomatoes, cut into slices
- 1 cucumber, diced
- 1/4 cup chopped fresh parsley or cilantro
- 2 tablespoons olive oil
- 1 tablespoon lemon juice
- Salt and pepper to taste

Steps for Cooking:

1. Rinse the quinoa under cold water and drain. Combine the quinoa and water in a saucepan. Bring to a boil, then reduce heat to low, cover, and simmer for about 15 minutes, until the quinoa is tender and the water is absorbed. Remove from heat and let it cool.
2. Combine the cooked quinoa, tomatoes, diced cucumber, and chopped fresh parsley or cilantro
in a large mixing bowl.
3. Whisk the olive oil, lemon juice, salt, and pepper in a small bowl to make the dressing.
4. Pour the dressing over the quinoa salad and toss gently to coat all ingredients evenly.

Servings 4	Prep time 15 Minutes	Cook time: 15 Minutes	Calories 220

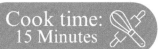

Fresh Salad

1 serving approximately:
2g protein 14g carbs
7g fat 0mg cholesterol
100mg sodium 300mg potassium

Ingredients:

- 1 cup strawberries, sliced
- 1 cup cherry tomatoes, halved
- 1 cup radishes, sliced
- 2 kiwis, peeled and sliced
- 1 cup microgreens
- 2 tablespoons extra virgin olive oil
- 1 tablespoon balsamic vinegar
- Salt and pepper to taste

Steps for Cooking:

1. Combine the sliced strawberries, cherry tomatoes, radishes, kiwis, and microgreens in a large salad bowl.
2. To make the dressing, whisk together the extra virgin olive oil, balsamic vinegar, salt, and pepper in a small mixing bowl.
3. Pour the dressing over the salad and toss gently to evenly coat all the fruits and vegetables.
4. Serve the salad immediately as a refreshing and nutritious side dish or light meal.

Servings	Prep time 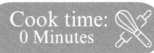	Cook time:	Calories
4	15 Minutes	0 Minutes	120

1 serving approximately:
2g protein 10g carbs
7g fat 0mg cholesterol
60mg sodium 400mg potassium

Cauliflower Rice Salad

Ingredients:

- 1 medium head cauliflower, grated into "rice."
- 1 tablespoon olive oil
- Zest and juice of 1 lemon
- 1 cup cherry tomatoes, halved
- 1 cucumber, diced
- 1/4 cup fresh parsley, chopped
- Salt and pepper to taste

Lemon Dressing:
- 3 tablespoons olive oil
- 2 tablespoons lemon juice
- 1 teaspoon Dijon mustard
- 1 teaspoon honey (optional)

Steps for Cooking:

1. Combine the grated cauliflower rice, halved cherry tomatoes, diced cucumber, and chopped parsley in a large mixing bowl.
2. In a separate small bowl, whisk together the olive oil, lemon juice, Dijon mustard, honey (if using), salt and pepper to make the lemon dressing.
3. Pour the lemon dressing over the cauliflower rice and vegetables. Toss well to coat everything evenly with the dressing.
4. Add the lemon zest to the salad and gently toss again. Season with additional salt and pepper to taste, if needed.

Servings	Prep time 	Cook time:	Calories
4	15 Minutes	0 Minutes	100

Tuna Salad

Ingredients:

- 2 cans (5 oz each) of tuna in water, drained
- 4 hard-boiled eggs, peeled and chopped
- 1 cucumber, diced
- 1 cup cherry tomatoes, halved
- 1/2 cup pitted olives, sliced
- 2 cups arugula or baby spinach
- 2 tablespoons extra virgin olive oil
- 1 tablespoon lemon juice
- Salt and pepper to taste

Steps for Cooking:

1. Combine the drained tuna, chopped hard-boiled eggs, diced cucumber, cherry tomatoes, sliced olives, and arugula or baby spinach in a large mixing bowl.
2. Whisk together the extra virgin olive oil, lemon juice, salt, and pepper in a small bowl to make the dressing.
3. Pour the dressing over the tuna and vegetable mixture, then toss gently until everything is well coated.
4. Divide the salad into serving bowls or plates.

1 serving approximately:
24g protein 8g carbs
18g fat 320mg cholesterol
580mg sodium 420mg potassium

| Servings 4 | Prep time 15 Minutes | Cook time: 0 Minutes | Calories 280 |

Shrimp and Persimmon Salad

Ingredients:

- 1 pound shrimp, peeled and deveined
- 2 persimmons, peeled and sliced
- 1 lemon, zest and juice
- 1/4 cup red onion, thinly sliced
- 4 cups lettuce, chopped
- 2 tablespoons Dijon mustard
- 2 tablespoons olive oil
- Salt and pepper to taste

Steps for Cooking:

1. Combine the shrimp with lemon zest in a bowl, a squeeze of lemon juice, salt, and pepper. Let it marinate for a few minutes.
2. Heat olive oil in a skillet over medium heat. Add the marinated shrimp and cook until pink and cooked through, about 3-4 minutes per side. Remove from heat and set aside.
3. Combine the chopped lettuce, sliced persimmons, thinly sliced red onion, and cooked shrimp in a large salad bowl.
4. To make the dressing, whisk together Dijon mustard, lemon juice, olive oil, salt, and pepper in a small bowl.
5. Pour the lemon-Dijon dressing over the salad and toss gently to coat everything evenly.

1 serving approximately:
25g protein 15g carbs
10g fat 150mg cholesterol
400mg sodium 600mg potassium

| Servings 4 | Prep time 15 Minutes | Cook time: 5 Minutes | Calories 250 |

Chapter 5: Soup Recipes

1 serving approximately:
3g protein 18g carbs
4g fat 0mg cholesterol
300mg sodium 700mg potassium

Roasted Red Pepper and Tomato Soup

Ingredients:

- 2 red bell peppers
- 4 large tomatoes
- 1 onion, chopped
- 2 cloves garlic, minced
- 2 cups low-sodium vegetable broth
- 1 teaspoon olive oil
- 1/2 teaspoon dried thyme
- Salt and pepper to taste
- Fresh rosemary for garnish
- Optional: Greek yogurt or coconut cream for serving

Steps for Cooking:

1. Preheat the oven to 400°F (200°C). Line a baking sheet with parchment paper.

2. Cut the red bell peppers in half, remove the seeds and membranes, place them on the prepared baking sheet, cut side down. Cut the tomatoes in half, put them on the same baking sheet, cut side up.

3. Drizzle the olive oil over the peppers and tomatoes. Roast in the oven for about 20-25 minutes until the peppers are charred and the tomatoes are softened.

4. Remove the baking sheet from the oven and let the peppers and tomatoes cool slightly. Peel the skin off the peppers and chop them into smaller pieces. Roughly chop the roasted tomatoes.

5. In a large pot, heat olive oil over medium heat. Add the chopped onion and garlic, and sauté until they become translucent.

6. Add the chopped roasted peppers and tomatoes to the pot. Stir in the dried thyme, salt, and pepper.

7. Pour in the vegetable broth and bring the mixture to a simmer. Cook for about 10-15 minutes, stirring occasionally.

8. Use an immersion blender to puree the soup until smooth. Alternatively, transfer the soup to a blender, blend until soft, then return it to the pot. Taste the soup and adjust the seasoning if needed. Add more vegetable broth or water to reach your desired consistency if the soup is too thick. Serve hot, garnished with fresh rosemary. Before serving, swirl in some Greek yogurt or coconut cream optionally.

Servings 4   Prep time 10 Minutes   Cook time: 30 Minutes    Calories 120

Cold Summer Soup

Ingredients:

- 2 large cucumbers, peeled and diced
- 1 cup radishes, diced
- 1 medium potato, peeled, boiled, and diced
- 4 hard-boiled eggs, peeled and chopped
- 1 cup cooked chicken, diced
- 1 cup plain yogurt
- 2 green onions, finely chopped
- 1/4 cup fresh dill, chopped
- Salt and pepper to taste
- 2 cups buttermilk
- Ice cubes (optional for chilling)

Steps for Cooking:

1. Combine diced cucumbers, radishes, boiled potatoes, chopped hard-boiled eggs, diced chicken, chopped green onions, and fresh dill in a large bowl.
2. Add plain yogurt to the bowl and mix well to combine all the ingredients.
3. Pour buttermilk into the bowl and stir until the soup reaches your desired consistency. Add more buttermilk if a thinner consistency is preferred.
4. Season the soup with salt and pepper to taste. Mix everything thoroughly.
5. Cover the bowl and refrigerate the Cold Soup for at least 1 hour to chill and allow the flavors to meld. Serve the Cold Soup in bowls. Add a few ice cubes to each serving.

1 serving approximately:
20g protein 22g carbs
12g fat 245mg cholesterol
550mg sodium 650mg potassium

Servings	Prep time	Cook time:	Calories
4	20 Minutes	10 Minutes	280

White Salmon Chowder

1 serving approximately:
27g protein 24g carbs
13g fat 70mg cholesterol
380mg sodium 780mg potassium

Ingredients:

- 1 lb fresh salmon fillet
- 1 tablespoon unsalted butter
- 1 onion, finely chopped
- 2 cloves garlic, minced
- 2 medium-sized potatoes, peeled and diced
- 2 celery stalks, diced
- 1 cup cauliflower florets
- 4 cups low-sodium chicken or vegetable broth
- 1 cup whole milk
- 1 teaspoon dried thyme
- green onions, thinly sliced
- 1 lemon, cut into wedges

Steps for Cooking:

1. In a large pot, melt unsalted butter over medium heat. Add chopped onion, minced garlic, and sauté until softened and fragrant, about 3-4 minutes.
2. Add diced potatoes, celery, and cauliflower to the pot. Cook for another 5 minutes, stirring occasionally.
3. Pour in the low-sodium chicken or vegetable broth. Bring the mixture to a boil, then reduce heat to low and let it simmer for 15 minutes or until the vegetables are tender.
4. Add the bite-sized salmon pieces and dried thyme to the chowder. Simmer gently until the salmon is cooked and flakes easily with a fork, about 5-7 minutes. Stir in the whole milk and continue simmering for 2-3 minutes.
5. Season the chowder with salt and white pepper according to your taste preferences.
6. Ladle the heart-healthy white salmon chowder into serving bowls. Garnish each bowl with thinly sliced green onions. Serve hot with lemon wedges on the side.

Servings	Prep time	Cook time:	Calories
4	15 Minutes	25 Minutes	320

Beef and Vegetable Soup

Ingredients:

- 1 lb lean beef stew meat, cut into bite-sized pieces
- 1 tablespoon olive oil
- 1 onion, chopped
- 2 cloves garlic, minced
- 2 carrots, peeled and sliced
- 1 large potato, peeled and diced
- 1 cup corn kernels (fresh or frozen)
- 1 cup diced sweet potato
- 6 cups low-sodium beef or vegetable broth
- 1 teaspoon dried thyme
- Fresh parsley, chopped

Steps for Cooking:

1. In a large pot, heat olive oil over medium heat. Add chopped onion and minced garlic and sauté until translucent and fragrant, about 3-4 minutes.
2. Add the beef stew meat to the pot and brown it on all sides for about 5-7 minutes. Stir in the sliced carrots, diced potato, corn kernels, and diced sweet potato.
3. Pour in the low-sodium beef or vegetable broth. Add dried thyme, salt, and pepper to taste. Bring the soup to a boil, then reduce the heat to low. Cover and simmer for 30 minutes or until the beef and vegetables are tender.
4. Taste and adjust seasoning if needed. Remove from heat. Garnish with chopped fresh parsley.

1 serving approximately:
5g protein 20g carbs
5g fat 5mg cholesterol
200mg sodium 400mg potassium

Servings 4	Prep time 15 Minutes	Cook time: 40 Minutes	Calories 290

1 serving approximately:
27g protein 24g carbs
13g fat 70mg cholesterol
380mg sodium 780mg potassium

Creamy Mushroom Soup

Ingredients:

- 1 tablespoon olive oil
- 1 small onion, diced
- 2 cloves garlic, minced
- 12 ounces mushrooms (button or cremini)
- 2 cups low-sodium vegetable broth
- 1 cup low-fat milk
- 2 tablespoons all-purpose flour
- Microgreens

Steps for Cooking:

1. In a large pot, heat the olive oil over medium heat. Add the diced onion and garlic, and sauté until softened and fragrant.
2. Add the sliced mushrooms to the pot and cook until they release moisture and brown, about 8-10 minutes. Pull out a few slices of mushrooms to serve and set aside.
3. Sprinkle the flour over the mushrooms and stir well to coat. Cook for another 2 minutes to remove the raw flour taste.
4. Pour in the low-sodium vegetable broth and stir to combine. Bring the mixture to a simmer.

5. Add the low-fat milk to the pot, stirring continuously to avoid lumps. Let the soup simmer gently for about 10 minutes until it thickens slightly. Season the soup with salt and pepper. Remove the pot from heat and let the soup cool slightly.
6. Use an immersion blender to puree until smooth and creamy. Return the pureed soup to the pot and reheat gently if needed. Serve the mushroom soup hot, garnished with fried mushroom slices and microgreens.

Servings 4	Prep time 10 Minutes	Cook time: 25 Minutes	Calories 150

Cauliflower Soup with Meatballs

Ingredients:

- 1 lb ground chicken breast
- 1/2 cup breadcrumbs
- 1 egg
- 2 tablespoons chopped fresh parsley
- Salt and pepper to taste
- 1 head cauliflower, chopped
- 1 onion, chopped
- 2 carrots, peeled and diced
- 2 celery stalks, diced
- 4 cups low-sodium chicken broth
- 1/2 teaspoon dried thyme
- 1/2 teaspoon dried oregano
- 1/2 cup low-fat milk or almond milk
- Fresh parsley, chopped

Steps for Cooking:

1. Mix ground chicken, breadcrumbs, egg, chopped parsley, salt, and pepper in a bowl. Form the mixture into small meatballs.
2. In a large pot, heat olive oil over medium heat. Add chopped onion, diced carrots, and diced celery. Sauté until vegetables are tender, about 5-7 minutes. Add cauliflower florets to the pot and sauté for 3-4 minutes.
3. Pour in low-sodium chicken broth, add dried thyme and oregano. Bring to a boil, then reduce heat to low and simmer for 10 minutes or until cauliflower is tender.
4. Meanwhile, cook the chicken meatballs in a separate pan until browned and cooked through. Transfer chicken meatballs to the soup pot. Stir in low-fat milk or almond milk. Simmer for another 5 minutes to allow flavors to meld together. Taste and adjust seasoning if needed. Garnish with chopped parsley.

1 serving approximately:
30g protein 20g carbs
10g fat 80mg cholesterol
500mg sodium 800mg potassium

Servings 4

Prep time 20 Minutes

Cook time: 25 Minutes

Calories 290

Ukrainian Borsch

Ingredients:

- 1 lb lean beef, cubed
- 1 onion, chopped
- 2 carrots, peeled and diced
- 2 beets, peeled and grated
- 2 potatoes, peeled and cubed
- 4 cups low-sodium beef broth
- 1 can (14.5 oz) diced tomatoes
- 1/4 head cabbage, shredded
- 2 tablespoons olive oil
- 2 cloves garlic, minced
- 2 bay leaves
- Fresh dill, chopped
- Low-fat sour cream

Steps for Cooking:

1. In a large pot, heat olive oil over medium heat. Add chopped onion, diced carrots, and minced garlic. Sauté until vegetables are tender, about 5-7 minutes. Add cubed lean beef to the pot and brown on all sides.
2. Pour in low-sodium beef broth and bring to a boil. Reduce heat to low, cover, and simmer for 20 minutes.
3. Add grated beets, cubed potatoes, diced tomatoes with their juices, shredded cabbage, bay leaves, salt, and pepper to the pot. Stir well to combine.
4. Cover and simmer for 15-20 minutes until all the vegetables are tender and the flavors are blended. Taste and adjust seasoning if needed.
5. Remove bay leaves before serving. Garnish with chopped fresh dill and a dollop of low-fat sour cream on top.

1 serving approximately:
25g protein 30g carbs
10g fat 60mg cholesterol
500mg sodium 12000mg potassium

Servings 4

Prep time 20 Minutes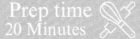

Cook time: 40 Minutes

Calories 300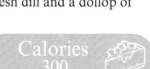

Spicy Pumpkin Soup

Ingredients:

- 2 cups pumpkin puree
- 1 small onion, chopped
- 2 cloves garlic, minced
- 1 tablespoon olive oil
- 4 cups low-sodium vegetable broth
- 1 teaspoon ground cumin
- 1/2 teaspoon ground coriander
- 1/4 teaspoon cayenne pepper (adjust to taste)
- Salt and black pepper to taste
- 1/2 cup plain Greek yogurt
- 1 cup whole wheat bread, cubed
- 1 tablespoon olive oil
- Pumpkin seeds (for garnish)

Steps for Cooking:

1. Heat 1 tablespoon of olive oil in a large pot over medium heat. Add the chopped onion, minced garlic, and sauté until softened for 3-4 minutes.
2. Stir in the pumpkin puree, ground cumin, coriander, cayenne pepper, salt, and black pepper. Cook for another 2-3 minutes for the flavors to meld together.
3. Pour in the low-sodium vegetable broth and bring the mixture to a boil. Reduce heat to low, cover, and let it simmer for 20 minutes.
4. While the soup is simmering, prepare the whole wheat croutons. Preheat the oven to 375°F (190°C).

5. Toss the cubed whole wheat bread with 1 tablespoon of olive oil and spread them on a baking sheet. Bake for 10-12 minutes until golden and crispy. After the soup has simmered, use an immersion blender and blend until smooth and creamy. Serve the pumpkin soup hot, garnished with a dollop of plain Greek yogurt, croutons, and pumpkin seeds.

1 serving approximately:
5g protein 25g carbs
7g fat 0mg cholesterol
200mg sodium 400mg potassium

Servings 	Prep time 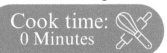	Cook time:	Calories
4	15 Minutes	30 Minutes	180

Cold Beet Soup

1 serving approximately:
8g protein 15g carbs
3g fat 110mg cholesterol
180mg sodium 400mg potassium

Ingredients:

- 2 cups cooked and peeled beets, diced
- 1 cucumber, peeled and diced
- 1 cup plain Greek yogurt
- 1 cup low-fat buttermilk
- 1 tablespoon lemon juice
- 2 cloves garlic, minced
- 1 tablespoon honey
- 2 hard-boiled eggs, halved
- Fresh green onions
- Fresh dill, chopped

Steps for Cooking:

1. Combine the diced beets, cucumber, plain Greek yogurt, low-fat buttermilk, minced garlic, lemon juice, honey, salt, and pepper in a blender.
2. Blend until smooth and well combined. Add a little water or extra buttermilk to reach your desired consistency if the soup is too thick. Transfer the blended mixture to a large bowl. Cover and refrigerate for at least 1 hour to chill thoroughly. Once chilled, stir the soup and taste to adjust the seasoning if needed. Add half a hard-boiled egg to each bowl, chopped fresh green onions and dill for garnish.

Servings	Prep time	Cook time:	Calories
4	15 Minutes	0 Minutes	120

1 serving approximately:
25g protein 10g carbs
25g fat 85mg cholesterol
250mg sodium 300mg potassium

Pomegranate Glazed Duck Breast

Ingredients:

- 4 duck breasts, skin on
- Salt and black pepper to taste
- 1/2 cup pomegranate juice
- 2 tablespoons honey
- 1 tablespoon balsamic vinegar
- 1 teaspoon grated ginger
- 2 cloves garlic, minced
- 1 teaspoon cornstarch (optional for thickening)
- mixed peppercorns

Steps for Cooking:

1. Preheat your oven to 375°F (190°C).
2. Score the skin of the duck breasts in a criss-cross pattern, being careful not to cut into the flesh. Season both sides of the duck breasts generously with salt and black pepper.
3. Heat a large, oven-safe skillet over medium-high heat. Once hot, add the duck breasts skin-side down and cook for about 5 minutes until the skin is golden brown and crispy. Flip the duck breasts over and cook for another 2 minutes.
4. While the duck breasts are cooking, prepare the glaze. Combine the pomegranate juice, honey, balsamic vinegar, grated ginger, and minced garlic in a small saucepan. Bring the mixture to a simmer over medium heat and cook for about 5-7 minutes until slightly thickening. If desired, mix in the cornstarch slurry to thicken the glaze further.

5. Brush the duck breasts generously with the pomegranate glaze, reserving some for serving. Sprinkle the duck with the peppercorns. Transfer the skillet to the preheated oven and roast for 8-10 minutes for medium-rare or until desired doneness. Remove the duck breasts from the oven and let them rest for a few minutes before slicing. Serve the sliced duck breasts drizzled with the remaining pomegranate glaze.

Servings
4

Prep time
15 Minutes

Cook time:
25 Minutes

Calories
380

Tomato Meat Balls

Ingredients:

- 1 pound lean ground beef
- 1/4 cup whole wheat bread crumbs
- 1/4 cup grated Parmesan cheese
- 1 egg, beaten
- 1/4 cup chopped fresh parsley
- 1/2 teaspoon garlic powder
- 1/2 teaspoon onion powder
- Salt and black pepper to taste
- 1 tablespoon olive oil
- 1 can (14 ounces) crushed tomatoes
- 1 teaspoon Italian seasoning
- 1/2 teaspoon honey (optional)
- Fresh parsley for garnish

Steps for Cooking:

1. Preheat the oven to 400°F (200°C). Line a baking sheet with parchment paper.
2. Combine ground beef, bread crumbs, Parmesan cheese, beaten egg, chopped parsley, garlic powder, onion powder, salt, and black pepper in a large bowl. Mix well until all ingredients are evenly incorporated.
3. Shape the mixture into meatballs about 1 inch in diameter. Place them on the prepared baking sheet. Bake the meatballs in the oven for 15-20 minutes or until cooked and browned. In a saucepan, heat olive oil over medium heat.

1 serving approximately:
25g protein 15g carbs
18g fat 80mg cholesterol
480mg sodium 500mg potassium

4. Add crushed tomatoes, Italian seasoning, and honey (if using).
5. Stir well and simmer for about 5 minutes. Add the baked meatballs to the tomato sauce in the saucepan. Gently coat the meatballs with the sauce and simmer for 5 minutes.

Servings	Prep time	Cook time:	Calories
4	15 Minutes	25 Minutes	320

Chicken Strips

1 serving approximately:
32g protein 14g carbs
14g fat 140mg cholesterol
480mg sodium 380mg potassium

Ingredients:

- 1 lb boneless, skinless chicken breasts cut into strips
- 1/2 cup whole wheat breadcrumbs
- 1/4 cup ground flaxseed
- 1 teaspoon paprika
- 1/2 teaspoon garlic powder
- 1/2 teaspoon onion powder
- 1/2 teaspoon dried oregano
- 1/2 teaspoon salt
- 1/4 teaspoon black pepper
- 2 eggs, beaten

Steps for Cooking:

1. Preheat the oven to 400°F (200°C). Line a baking sheet with parchment paper and set aside.
2. Mix the whole wheat breadcrumbs, ground flaxseed, paprika, garlic powder, onion powder, dried oregano, salt, and black pepper in a shallow dish
3. Dip each chicken strip into the beaten eggs, allowing excess to drip off, then coat both sides in the breadcrumb mixture, pressing gently to adhere.
4. Place the coated chicken strips on the prepared baking sheet.

5. Bake in the oven for 12-15 minutes or until the chicken is cooked and the coating is crispy and golden brown.

Servings	Prep time	Cook time:	Calories
4	10 Minutes	15 Minutes	320

Black Bean & Turkey Chili

Ingredients:

- 1 tablespoon olive oil
- 1 lb ground turkey
- 1 small onion, diced
- 2 cloves garlic, minced
- 1 medium sweet potato
- 1 bell pepper, diced
- 1 can (15 oz) black beans
- 1 can (14.5 oz) diced tomatoes
- 1 cup low-sodium chicken broth
- 2 teaspoons chili powder
- 1 teaspoon ground cumin
- 1/2 teaspoon paprika

Steps for Cooking:

1. Heat olive oil over medium heat in a large pot or Dutch oven. Add ground turkey and cook until browned, breaking it apart with a spoon, about 5-7 minutes.
2. Add diced onion and minced garlic to the pot. Cook for another 2-3 minutes until onions are softened.
3. Stir in diced sweet potato and bell pepper, cooking for 5 minutes until slightly softened.
4. Add black beans, diced tomatoes, chicken broth, chili powder, cumin, paprika, salt, and black pepper to the pot. Bring the chili to a simmer, then reduce heat to low and let it cook, covered, for about 20 minutes, stirring occasionally.

1 serving approximately:
27g protein 32g carbs
15g fat 65mg cholesterol
480mg sodium 780mg potassium

Servings 4 | **Prep time** 15 Minutes | **Cook time:** 30 Minutes | **Calories** 380

Stuffed Chicken Breast

1 serving approximately:
42g protein 2g carbs
15g fat 120mg cholesterol
350mg sodium 580mg potassium

Ingredients:

- 4 boneless, skinless chicken breasts
- 1 cup fresh spinach leaves
- 1/2 cup crumbled feta cheese
- 2 cloves garlic, minced
- 1 tablespoon olive oil
- 1 teaspoon dried oregano
- Salt and black pepper to taste
- Toothpicks

Steps for Cooking:

1. Preheat the oven to 375°F (190°C). Grease a baking dish with cooking spray and set aside.
2. In a skillet, heat olive oil over medium heat. Add minced garlic and sauté until fragrant, about 1 minute.
3. Add fresh spinach leaves to the skillet and cook until wilted, about 2-3 minutes. Remove from heat and let cool slightly.
4. Make a horizontal slit in each chicken breast to create a pocket, being careful not to cut all the way through. Season the inside of the pockets with dried oregano, salt, and black pepper.
5. Stuff each chicken breast with equal amounts of cooked spinach and crumbled feta cheese. Secure the openings with toothpicks.
6. Place the stuffed chicken breasts in the prepared baking dish and bake in the oven for 20-25 minutes until the chicken is cooked and no longer pink in the center.

Servings 4 | **Prep time** 15 Minutes 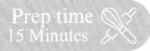 | **Cook time:** 25 Minutes  | **Calories** 320

Grilled Chicken Tabaka

Ingredients:

- 1 whole chicken (about 3-4 pounds), butterflied
- 2 tablespoons olive oil
- 4 cloves garlic, minced
- 1 tablespoon lemon juice
- 1 teaspoon ground cumin
- 1 teaspoon smoked paprika
- 1/2 teaspoon ground black pepper
- 1/2 teaspoon salt
- Fresh parsley for garnish

Steps for Cooking:

1. Preheat the oven to 375°F. In a small bowl, mix olive oil, garlic, lemon juice, cumin, smoked paprika, black pepper, and salt. Rub the mixture all over the butterflied chicken, ensuring it is well coated.

2. Heat a large oven-safe skillet over medium-high heat. Place the chicken in the skillet, skin side down, and press it flat with a heavy pan or a foil-wrapped brick. Cook for about 5 minutes until the skin is browned.

3. Flip the chicken over, transfer the skillet to the oven, and bake for 25 minutes, or until the internal temperature reaches 165°F. Remove from the oven and let rest for 5 minutes and garnish with fresh parsley.

1 serving approximately:
30g protein 0g carbs
22g fat 80mg cholesterol
380mg sodium 350mg potassium

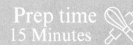 **Servings** 4

 **Prep time** 15 Minutes

Cook time: 20 Minutes

Calories 320

Eggplant Boats with Meat

1 serving approximately:
25g protein 20g carbs
12g fat 60mg cholesterol
350mg sodium 700mg potassium

Ingredients:

- 2 large eggplants
- 1/2 pound lean ground beef or turkey
- 1 small onion, finely chopped
- 2 cloves garlic, minced
- 1 teaspoon ground cumin
- 1 teaspoon paprika
- Salt and black pepper to taste
- 1 tablespoon olive oil
- 1 cup tomato sauce
- 1/4 cup low-fat mozzarella cheese, shredded

Steps for Cooking:

1. Preheat the oven to 375°F (190°C). Grease a baking dish with olive oil.

2. Cut the eggplants in half lengthwise and scoop out the flesh using a spoon, leaving about 1/4-inch thick shells. Chop the scooped-out flesh and set aside.

3. In a skillet, heat olive oil over medium heat. Add chopped onion and minced garlic, and sauté until translucent.

4. Add the ground meat to the skillet and cook until browned, breaking it up with a spoon as it cooks. Stir in the chopped eggplant flesh, ground cumin, paprika, salt, and black pepper.

5. Cook for another 5 minutes until the eggplant is tender. Place the hollowed eggplant boats in the prepared baking dish. Spoon the meat mixture evenly into each ship. Pour tomato sauce over the eggplant boats, covering them evenly. Cover the baking dish with foil and bake in the oven for 25-30 minutes until the eggplant is tender. Remove the foil, sprinkle shredded mozzarella cheese over the top of each boat, and bake uncovered for an additional 5 minutes until the cheese is melted.

 Servings 4

 **Prep time** 25 Minutes

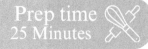 **Cook time:** 35 Minutes

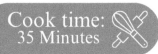 **Calories** 300

Baked Pork

1 serving approximately:
30g protein 2g carbs
14g fat 75mg cholesterol
400mg sodium 500mg potassium

Ingredients:

- 1 pound lean pork loin, sliced into 1-inch thick pieces
- 2 tablespoons olive oil
- 1 teaspoon paprika
- 1 teaspoon garlic powder
- 1 teaspoon onion powder
- 1/2 teaspoon ground cumin
- Salt and black pepper to taste
- Fresh parsley or cilantro

Steps for Cooking:

1. Preheat the oven to 400°F (200°C). Grease a baking dish with olive oil.
2. Mix paprika, garlic powder, onion powder, ground cumin, salt, and black pepper in a small bowl.
3. Rub the spice mixture evenly over the pork loin slices, ensuring they are well coated.
4. Place the seasoned pork slices in the prepared baking dish.
5. Drizzle olive oil over the pork slices to keep them moist during baking.
6. Bake in the preheated oven for 25-30 minutes or until the pork is cooked through and tender.
7. Remove from the oven and let it rest for a few minutes before serving. Garnish with fresh parsley or cilantro before serving.

Servings	Prep time 	Cook time:	Calories
4	15 Minutes	30 Minutes	250

Filet Mignon

Ingredients:

- 2 filet mignon steaks (6-8 ounces each)
- Salt and black pepper to taste
- 1 tablespoon olive oil
- 1 bunch asparagus, trimmed
- 1 tablespoon pink peppercorns, crushed
- 2 cloves garlic, minced
- 1 tablespoon balsamic vinegar
- Fresh parsley for garnish

Steps for Cooking:

1. Preheat the oven to 400°F (200°C).
2. Season the filet mignon steaks with salt and black pepper on both sides.
3. In an oven-safe skillet, heat olive oil over medium-high heat. Sear the steaks for 2-3 minutes on each side until browned.
4. Transfer the skillet to the preheated oven and roast the steaks for about 8-10 minutes for medium-rare doneness or longer, according to your preference. Remove the steaks from the skillet and let them rest for a few minutes.
5. In the same skillet, add the trimmed asparagus and minced garlic. Sauté for 4-5 minutes until the asparagus is tender-crisp.
6. Add crushed pink peppercorns and balsamic vinegar to the skillet. Stir to coat the asparagus evenly with the flavors. To serve, place a bed of cooked asparagus on each plate. Top with the roasted filet mignon steaks. Garnish with fresh parsley and additional pink peppercorns if desired.

1 serving approximately:
35g protein 10g carbs
18g fat 90mg cholesterol
300mg sodium 800mg potassium

Servings	Prep time 	Cook time: 	Calories
4	15 Minutes	20 Minutes	350

Chicken Thighs

Ingredients:

- 4 boneless, skinless chicken thighs
- 1 cup plain Greek yogurt
- 2 tablespoons olive oil
- 2 tablespoons lemon juice
- 2 garlic cloves, minced
- 1 teaspoon dried oregano
- 1 teaspoon dried thyme
- Salt and pepper to taste
- Fresh parsley for garnish (optional)

Steps for Cooking:

1. Combine Greek yogurt, olive oil, lemon juice, minced garlic, dried oregano, dried thyme, salt, and pepper in a bowl. Mix well to make the marinade.
2. Place the chicken thighs in a resealable plastic bag or shallow dish. Pour the marinade over the chicken, ensuring each piece is well coated. Seal the bag or cover the dish and refrigerate for at least 2 hours, preferably overnight.
3. Preheat the grill or oven to medium-high heat.

4. Remove the chicken from the marinade and shake off excess. Discard the remaining marinade. Grill the chicken thighs for about 5-7 minutes per side, or until cooked through and the juices run clear. If using the oven, bake at 400°F (200°C) for 20-25 minutes, or until done. Remove the chicken from the grill or oven and let it rest for a few minutes before serving. If desired, garnish with fresh parsley, and serve hot with your favorite sides.

1 serving approximately:
25g protein 5g carbs
15g fat 90mg cholesterol
300mg sodium 350mg potassium

 Servings 4

 Prep time 15 Minutes

 Cook time: 25 Minutes

 Calories 250

1 serving approximately:
28g protein 12g carbs
13g fat 120mg cholesterol
500mg sodium 350mg potassium

Asian Turkey Meatloaf

Ingredients:

- 1 lb ground turkey
- 1/2 cup whole wheat breadcrumbs
- 1/4 cup low-sodium soy sauce
- 1/4 cup chopped green onions
- 2 tablespoons grated ginger
- 2 tablespoons sesame oil
- 1 tablespoon honey
- 1 tablespoon rice vinegar
- 1 egg
- Salt and pepper to taste
- Sesame seeds for garnish

Steps for Cooking:

1. Preheat the oven to 375°F (190°C). Grease a loaf pan with cooking spray.
2. Combine ground turkey, whole wheat breadcrumbs, soy sauce, green onions, grated ginger, sesame oil, honey, rice vinegar, egg, salt, and pepper in a large mixing bowl. Mix until well combined.
3. Transfer the turkey mixture to the greased loaf pan, pressing it down evenly.
4. Sprinkle sesame seeds on top of the meatloaf.

5. Bake in the oven for about 40-45 minutes or until the internal temperature reaches 165°F (74°C).

6. Remove the meatloaf from the oven and let it rest for 5-10 minutes before slicing.

7. Slice the meatloaf and serve with steamed vegetables or a side salad.

 Servings 4

Prep time 15 Minutes

 Cook time: 45 Minutes

 Calories 280

Coconut Chicken Curry

Ingredients:

- 1 lb boneless, skinless chicken breasts cut into bite-sized pieces
- 2 tablespoons olive oil
- 1 onion, finely chopped
- 3 cloves garlic, minced
- 1 tablespoon grated fresh ginger
- 2 teaspoons ground turmeric
- 1 teaspoon ground cumin
- 1 teaspoon ground coriander
- 1/2 teaspoon paprika
- 1/4 teaspoon cayenne pepper (optional)
- 1 can (14 oz) coconut milk
- 1 cup low-sodium chicken broth
- 2 cups chopped vegetables (such as bell peppers, carrots, and peas)
- Salt and black pepper to taste
- Fresh parsley, chopped, for garnish (optional)

Steps for Cooking:

1. In a large skillet, heat olive oil over medium heat. Add chopped onion and cook until softened, about 3-4 minutes.
2. Add minced garlic and grated ginger to the skillet, cooking for another minute until fragrant.
3. Stir in ground turmeric, ground cumin, coriander, paprika, and cayenne pepper (if used), cooking for 1-2 minutes until spices are toasted.
4. Add chicken pieces to the skillet and cook until browned on all sides, about 5-7 minutes.
5. Pour in coconut milk and chicken broth, stirring to combine. Bring the mixture to a simmer, then reduce heat to low and let it simmer for 10-12 minutes.
6. Add chopped vegetables to the skillet and cook for another 5-7 minutes, or until vegetables are tender and chicken is cooked through.
7. Season the curry with salt and black pepper to taste. If desired, garnish with chopped fresh parsley.

1 serving approximately:
28g protein 20g carbs
20g fat 65mg cholesterol
400mg sodium 600mg potassium

 Servings 4

 Prep time 15 Minutes

 Cook time: 25 Minutes

 Calories 380

Lamb Kabobs

Ingredients:

- 1 lb lamb loin, cut into cubes
- 1 tablespoon olive oil
- 2 cloves garlic, minced
- 1 teaspoon ground cumin
- 1 teaspoon ground coriander
- ·1/2 teaspoon smoked paprika
- 1/2 teaspoon ground cinnamon
- 1/4 teaspoon ground ginger
- 1/4 teaspoon cayenne pepper
- Salt and black pepper to taste
- 1/4 cup plain Greek yogurt
- 1 tablespoon lemon juice
- 1 tablespoon chopped mint
- Skewers

Steps for Cooking:

1. In a bowl, add olive oil, minced garlic, cumin, coriander, paprika, cinnamon, ginger, cayenne pepper, salt, and black pepper. Add lamb cubes and toss to coat evenly. Marinate for at least 30 minutes or overnight in the refrigerator.
2. Preheat the grill or grill pan over medium-high heat. Thread marinate lamb cubes onto skewers.
3. Grill the lamb kabobs for 10-12 minutes, turning occasionally, until cooked to the desired doneness.
4. To make the yogurt sauce, mix Greek yogurt, lemon juice, and chopped mint in a small bowl.

1 serving approximately:
29g protein 2g carbs
30g fat 95mg cholesterol
120mg sodium 350mg potassium

| Servings 4 | Prep time 15 Minutes  | Cook time: 15 Minutes | Calories 390 |

Meatball Curry

1 serving approximately:
25g protein 15g carbs
20g fat 95mg cholesterol
480mg sodium 450mg potassium

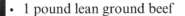

Ingredients:

- 1 pound lean ground beef
- 1/2 cup whole wheat breadcrumbs
- 1/4 cup finely chopped onion
- 1 teaspoon minced garlic
- 1 egg
- 1 teaspoon curry powder
- Salt and pepper to taste
- 1 tablespoon olive oil
- 1 can (14 oz) diced tomatoes
- 1 teaspoon paprika
- Fresh cilantro

Steps for Cooking:

1. Combine the ground beef, breadcrumbs, onion, garlic, egg, curry powder, salt, and pepper in a mixing bowl. Mix well and form into meatballs
2. Preheat a grill or grill pan over medium-high heat. Grill the meatballs for about 10-12 minutes, turning occasionally, until cooked through and browned on all sides.
3. In a saucepan, heat olive oil over medium heat. Add the diced tomatoes, paprika, salt, and pepper. Cook for 5-7 minutes, stirring occasionally, until the sauce thickens slightly.

4. Place the grilled meatballs in the curry tomato sauce, coating them evenly. Simmer for an additional 5 minutes. Serve the grilled beef meatballs with curry tomato sauce garnished with fresh cilantro.

| Servings 4  | Prep time 20 Minutes  | Cook time: 25 Minutes | Calories 340 |

Chicken Liver

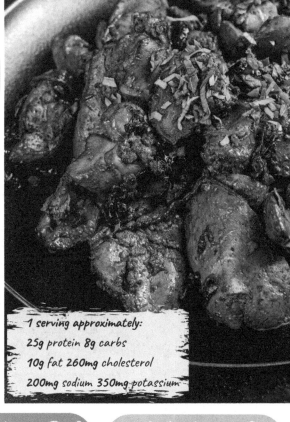

1 serving approximately:
25g protein 8g carbs
10g fat 260mg cholesterol
200mg sodium 350mg potassium

Ingredients:

- 1 pound chicken livers, cleaned and trimmed
- Salt and black pepper to taste
- 2 tablespoons olive oil
- 1 large onion, thinly sliced
- 2 cloves garlic, minced
- 1/2 teaspoon paprika
- 1/4 cup chopped fresh parsley
- Lemon wedges for serving

Steps for Cooking:

1. Season the chicken livers with salt and black pepper.
2. In a large skillet, heat olive oil over medium heat. Add the sliced onions and sauté until they become translucent and lightly browned, about 5-7 minutes.
3. Add minced garlic to the skillet and cook for another 1-2 minutes until fragrant.
4. Push the onions and garlic to the side of the skillet. Add the seasoned chicken livers to the center of the skillet and cook for about 4-5 minutes on each side until they are browned and cooked through.
. Sprinkle paprika over the chicken livers and onions, then stir to combine.
. Remove the skillet from heat and sprinkle chopped fresh parsley over the chicken liver mixture. Serve the chicken liver garnished with lemon wedges.

| Servings 4 | Prep time 10 Minutes  | Cook time: 20 Minutes | Calories 230 |

Stuffed Potato Boats

1 serving approximately:
25g protein 30g carbs
12g fat 60mg cholesterol
400mg sodium 800mg potassium

Ingredients:

- 4 large potatoes, scrubbed and halved lengthwise
- 1 pound lean ground beef or turkey
- 1 onion, finely chopped
- 2 cloves garlic, minced
- 1/2 cup diced tomatoes (canned or fresh)
- 1 teaspoon paprika
- Salt and black pepper to taste
- 2 tablespoons olive oil
- 1/4 cup chopped fresh parsley
- 4 slices of tomato (optional)
- 8-12 string beans, trimmed

Steps for Cooking:

1. Preheat the oven to 375°F (190°C).
2. Place the halved potatoes on a baking sheet. Using a spoon, scoop out the center of each potato half to create a hollow space for stuffing. Reserve the scooped-out potato flesh for another use.
3. In a skillet, heat olive oil over medium heat. Add chopped onion and minced garlic and sauté until softened and translucent, about 3-4 minutes.
4. Add the ground beef or turkey to the skillet and cook until browned, breaking it apart with a spoon as it cooks.
5. Stir in diced tomatoes, paprika, salt, and black pepper. Cook the meat mixture for another 5-7 minutes until the flavors meld together.
6. Fill each hollowed-out potato half with the minced meat stew mixture, pressing gently to pack it in. Top each stuffed potato half with a slice of tomato (if using) and arrange string beans around the potatoes on the baking sheet. Bake in the preheated oven for 25-30 minutes until the potatoes are tender and the filling is heated.

| Servings 4 | Prep time 20 Minutes  | Cook time: 40 Minutes 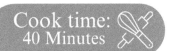 | Calories 350 |

Thai Chicken Satay

1 serving approximately:
28g protein 15g carbs
24g fat 65mg cholesterol
400mg sodium 450mg potassium

Ingredients:

- 1 lb boneless, skinless chicken breasts cut into strips
- 1/4 cup coconut milk
- Zest and juice of 1 lime
- 2 tablespoons low-sodium soy sauce
- 1 tablespoon honey
- 1 clove garlic, minced
- 1 teaspoon grated fresh ginger
- 1/4 teaspoon red pepper flakes
- 1/4 cup natural peanut butter
- 2 tablespoons low-sodium soy sauce
- 1 tablespoon honey
- 1 tablespoon lime juice
- 1/2 teaspoon grated ginger

Steps for Cooking:

1. Whisk together coconut milk, lime zest, lime juice, soy sauce, honey, minced garlic, grated ginger, and red pepper flakes (if using). Add chicken strips to the marinade, toss to coat, and let marinate for at least 15 minutes.

2. While the chicken is marinating, prepare the peanut sauce. Combine peanut butter, soy sauce, honey, lime juice, and grated ginger in another bowl. Stir until well combined, adding water as needed to reach the desired consistency. Set aside.

3. Preheat the grill or grill pan over medium-high heat. Thread marinated chicken strips onto soaked wooden skewers.

4. Lightly coat the grill or grill pan with cooking spray. Grill the chicken skewers on each side for 3-4 minutes until cooked through and slightly charred. For dipping, serve the chicken satay with the peanut sauce on the side.

Servings 4	Prep time 20 Minutes	Cook time: 15 Minutes	Calories 380

Stir Fry Noodles with Beef

1 serving approximately:
25g protein 40g carbs
10g fat 45mg cholesterol
400mg sodium 600mg potassium

Ingredients:

- ·8 ounces whole wheat noodles
- 8 ounces lean beef steak
- 1 tablespoon olive oil
- 1 red bell pepper, sliced
- 1 cup broccoli florets
- 2 cloves garlic, minced
- 1 teaspoon paprika
- 2 tablespoons low-sodium soy sauce
- 1 tablespoon sesame seeds

Steps for Cooking:

1. Cook the whole wheat noodles according to package instructions until al dente. Drain and set aside.

2. In a large skillet or wok, heat olive oil over medium-high heat. Add the thinly sliced beef and cook until browned and cooked through. Remove the meat from the skillet and set aside.

3. In the same skillet, add the sliced bell peppers and broccoli florets. Stir-fry for about 3-4 minutes. Add minced garlic and paprika to the vegetables. Season with salt and black pepper to taste.

4. Return the cooked beef to the skillet. Add the cooked noodles and low-sodium soy sauce. Toss everything together until well combined and heated through. Remove from heat and sprinkle toasted sesame seeds over the stir fry.

Servings 4	Prep time  15 Minutes	Cook time:  15 Minutes	Calories 350

Turkey Breast with Oranges

Ingredients:

- 1.5 pounds turkey breast, boneless and skinless
- 2 oranges, peeled and sliced
- 2 tablespoons olive oil
- 2 tablespoons honey
- 2 tablespoons low-sodium soy sauce
- 1 teaspoon grated ginger
- 2 cloves garlic, minced
- Salt and pepper to taste
- Fresh thyme for garnish

Steps for Cooking:

1. Preheat the oven to 375°F (190°C).
2. To make the marinade, whisk together olive oil, honey, soy sauce, grated ginger, minced garlic, salt, and pepper in a small bowl.
3. Place the turkey breast in a baking dish. Arrange the orange slices around and on top of the turkey.
4. Pour the marinade over the turkey and oranges, ensuring they are evenly coated.
5. Cover the baking dish with foil and bake for 25 minutes. Then, remove the foil and continue baking for another 10 minutes or until the turkey is cooked through and golden brown. Remove from the oven and let it rest for a few minutes before slicing. Garnish with fresh thyme before serving.

1 serving approximately:
30g protein 20g carbs
12g fat 80mg cholesterol
450mg sodium 380mg potassium

Servings	Prep time	Cook time:	Calories
4	15 Minutes	35 Minutes	320

Lamb Burgers

1 serving approximately:
25g protein 30g carbs
20g fat 75mg cholesterol
550mg sodium 450mg potassium

Ingredients:

- 1 lb ground lamb
- 1/4 cup finely chopped red onion
- 2 cloves garlic, minced
- 1 teaspoon dried oregano
- 1/2 teaspoon dried mint
- 1/2 teaspoon ground cumin
- 4 whole wheat burger buns
- 1 cup shredded lettuce
- 1 large tomato, sliced
- 1 yellow bell pepper, sliced
- 1/4 cup crumbled feta cheese

For Tzatziki Sauce:
- 1 cup plain Greek yogurt
- 1/2 cucumber
- 1 clove garlic, minced
- 1 tablespoon chopped fresh dill
- 1 tablespoon lemon juice

Steps for Cooking:

1. Combine ground lamb, chopped red onion, minced garlic, dried oregano, mint, ground cumin, salt, and black pepper in a mixing bowl. Mix until well combined.
2. Divide the mixture into 4 equal portions and shape each into a patty.
3. Preheat a grill or grill pan over medium-high heat. Grill the lamb burgers on each side for 5-6 minutes until they reach an internal temperature of 160°F (71°C).
4. While the burgers are cooking, prepare the tzatziki sauce. In a small bowl, combine Greek yogurt, grated cucumber, minced garlic, chopped fresh dill, lemon juice, salt, and black pepper. Stir well to combine.
5. Toast the whole wheat burger buns on the grill for a minute or until lightly browned. To assemble the burgers, place a lamb patty on each toasted bun. Top with shredded lettuce, sliced tomato, bell pepper, crumbled feta cheese, and a dollop of tzatziki sauce.

Servings	Prep time	Cook time:	Calories
4	15 Minutes	12 Minutes	420

1 serving approximately:
25g protein 2g carbs
10g fat 60mg cholesterol
300mg sodium 600mg potassium

Tuscan Style Grilled Octopus

Ingredients:

- 2 lbs octopus, cleaned and tenderized
- 1/4 cup olive oil
- 4 cloves garlic, minced
- 2 tablespoons fresh lemon juice
- 1 teaspoon dried oregano
- Salt and black pepper to taste
- Lemon wedges for serving
- Chopped fresh parsley for garnish

Steps for Cooking:

1. Preheat your grill to medium-high heat.
2. To make the marinade, mix olive oil, minced garlic, lemon juice, dried oregano, salt, and black pepper in a bowl.
3. Brush the octopus with the marinade mixture, ensuring it's evenly coated.
4. Place the octopus on the preheated grill and cook for about 15 minutes per side or until charred and tender. Cooking time may vary depending on the size of the octopus.
5. Remove the grilled octopus from the grill and let it rest for a few minutes before slicing it into serving portions.
6. Serve the octopus with Greek salad and lemon wedges and garnish with chopped fresh parsley.

 Servings
4

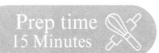 Prep time
15 Minutes

 Cook time:
30 Minutes

 Calories
200

Fish Meatballs

Ingredients:

- 1 pound white fish fillets, deboned and skinned
- 1 medium carrot, grated
- 1/2 cup whole wheat breadcrumbs
- 1 egg, beaten
- 2 garlic cloves, minced
- 1/4 cup chopped fresh parsley
- Salt and black pepper to taste
- 2 tablespoons olive oil
- 1 can (14 ounces) diced tomatoes
- 1/2 teaspoon dried oregano
- 1/2 teaspoon dried basil
- 1/4 teaspoon red pepper flakes (optional)
- Fresh basil leaves for garnish

Steps for Cooking:

1. In a food processor, pulse the white fish fillets until finely chopped.
2. Transfer the chopped fish to a mixing bowl and add grated carrot, breadcrumbs, beaten egg, minced garlic, chopped parsley, salt, and black pepper. Mix until well combined.
3. Shape the fish mixture into meatballs about 1 inch in diameter.
4. In a large skillet, heat olive oil over medium heat. Add the fish meatballs and cook until browned on all sides, about 5-7 minutes. Remove the meatballs from the skillet and set aside.
5. Add diced tomatoes, dried oregano, dried basil, and red pepper flakes in the same skillet. Bring to a simmer and cook for 5 minutes.
6. Return the fish meatballs to the skillet with the tomato sauce. Cover and simmer for 10 minutes or until the meatballs are cooked through.

1 serving approximately:
25g protein 15g carbs
10g fat 80mg cholesterol
350mg sodium 500mg potassium

Servings 4	Prep time 20 Minutes	Cook time: 25 Minutes	Calories 250

Sesame Tuna Steaks

1 serving approximately:
35g protein 10g carbs
15g fat 60mg cholesterol
300mg sodium 500mg potassium

Ingredients:

- 4 tuna steaks, about 6 oz each
- 2 tablespoons sesame seeds
- Salt and black pepper to taste
- 2 tablespoons olive oil
- Lemon wedges (for serving)

Steps for Cooking:

1. Season the tuna steaks with salt and black pepper on both sides.
2. Sprinkle sesame seeds on a plate and press the tuna steaks into the sesame seeds to coat them evenly.
3. In a large skillet, heat the olive oil over medium-high heat. Add the sesame-crusted tuna steaks and cook for 2-3 minutes per side for medium-rare doneness.
4. Remove the cooked tuna steaks from the skillet and place them on a serving plate.
8. Serve the sesame-crusted tuna steaks with the mixed salad.

Servings 4	Prep time 15 Minutes	Cook time: 10 Minutes	Calories 300

Garlic Butter Lobster Tails

Ingredients:

- 2 lobster tails (6-8 ounces each)
- 4 tablespoons unsalted butter, melted
- 3 cloves garlic, minced
- 1 tablespoon chopped fresh parsley
- Salt and pepper to taste
- Lemon wedges, for serving

Steps for Cooking:

1. Preheat your oven to 400°F (200°C). Line a baking sheet with parchment paper or foil.
2. Cut along the top of each lobster tail shell using kitchen shears, stopping at the tail. Carefully pull the meat from the shell, keeping it attached at the base.
3. Mix the melted butter, minced garlic, chopped parsley, salt, and pepper in a small bowl.
4. Brush the garlic butter mixture generously over the exposed lobster meat and inside the shell.
5. Place the lobster tails on the prepared baking sheet and bake in the oven for about 12-15 minutes or until the lobster meat is opaque and cooked through.
6. Serve the baked lobster tails hot with steamed asparagus and lemon wedges on the side.

1 serving approximately:
30g protein 1g carbs
18g fat 175mg cholesterol
450mg sodium 270mg potassium

 Servings 2   Prep time 15 Minutes   Cook time: 15 Minutes   Calories 280

1 serving approximately:
30g protein 12g carbs
15g fat 80mg cholesterol
500mg sodium 600mg potassium

Teriyaki Glazed Salmon

Ingredients:

- 4 salmon fillets, cut into pieces
- 1/4 cup low-sodium soy sauce
- 2 tablespoons honey
- 1 tablespoon rice vinegar
- 1 tablespoon sesame oil
- 2 cloves garlic, minced
- 1 teaspoon grated ginger
- 1 tablespoon cornstarch (optional, for thickening the sauce)
- Sesame seeds and chopped green onions for garnish

Steps for Cooking:

1. Preheat the oven to 400°F (200°C). Line a baking sheet with parchment paper or foil and lightly grease it.
2. Whisk together soy sauce, honey, rice vinegar, sesame oil, minced garlic and grated ginger to make the teriyaki glaze in a small bowl.
3. Place the salmon pieces on the prepared baking sheet. Brush each fillet generously with the teriyaki glaze, reserving some glaze for later.
4. Bake the salmon in the preheated oven for about 12-15 minutes or until the fish flakes easily with a fork.

5. Heat the remaining teriyaki glaze in a small saucepan over medium heat while the salmon is baking. If desired, add cornstarch mixed with water to thicken the glaze. Once the salmon is cooked, remove it from the oven and brush it with the heated teriyaki glaze. Sprinkle sesame seeds and chopped green onions over the salmon fillets before serving.

Servings 4   Prep time 10 Minutes   Cook time: 15 Minutes   Calories 300

Mediterranean Style Cod

Ingredients:

- 4 cod fillets (about 6 ounces each)
- 2 tablespoons olive oil
- 1 teaspoon dried oregano
- 1 teaspoon dried basil
- 1 teaspoon dried thyme
- 1/2 teaspoon garlic powder
- 1/2 teaspoon onion powder
- Salt and black pepper to taste
- 1 cup cherry tomatoes, halved
- 1 lemon, sliced
- 1/4 cup chopped fresh parsley, for garnish

Steps for Cooking:

1. Preheat the oven to 400°F (200°C). Lightly grease a baking dish with olive oil.
2. Pat the cod fillets dry with paper towels and place them in the prepared baking dish.
3. Mix olive oil, dried oregano, dried basil, dried thyme, garlic powder, onion powder, salt, and black pepper in a small bowl to make a seasoning mixture.
4. Brush the seasoning mixture over the cod fillets, ensuring they are evenly coated.
5. Place lemon slices and halved cherry tomatoes on the seasoned cod fillets.

6. Bake the cod in the preheated oven for about 15-20 minutes, or until the fish flakes easily with a fork and is cooked through. Remove the baked cod from the oven and garnish with chopped fresh parsley before serving.

1 serving approximately:
30g protein 3g carbs
12g fat 60mg cholesterol
400mg sodium 500mg potassium

Servings	Prep time	Cook time:	Calories
4	15 Minutes	20 Minutes	250

Spicy Stir-Fry Shrimps

1 serving approximately:
25g protein 15g carbs
10g fat 150mg cholesterol
400mg sodium 450mg potassium

Ingredients:

- 1 pound large shrimp
- 1 red bell pepper, thinly sliced
- 1 yellow bell pepper, thinly sliced
- 1 green bell pepper, thinly sliced
- 1 cup green peas, fresh or frozen
- 1 onion, thinly sliced
- 2 tablespoons olive oil
- 3 cloves garlic, minced
- 1 tablespoon grated ginger
- 1 teaspoon red pepper flakes (adjust to taste)
- 2 tablespoons low-sodium soy sauce
- 1 tablespoon sesame seeds
- Fresh cilantro for garnish

Steps for Cooking:

1. In a large skillet or wok, heat olive oil over medium-high heat. Add minced garlic, grated ginger, and red pepper flakes. Stir fry for about 30 seconds until fragrant.
2. Add sliced bell peppers, onion, and green peas to the skillet. Stir fry for 3-4 minutes until the vegetables are slightly tender yet crisp.
3. Push the vegetables to the side of the skillet and add the shrimp. Cook the shrimp on each side for 2-3 minutes until they turn pink and opaque.

4. Stir in low-sodium soy sauce, sesame seeds, salt, and pepper. Toss everything together to coat evenly. Cook for another 1-2 minutes, allowing the flavors to meld together. Remove from heat and garnish with fresh cilantro before serving.

Servings	Prep time	Cook time:	Calories
4	15 Minutes	10 Minutes	250

Scallops and Shrimp Delight

Ingredients:

- 1 pound sea scallops, rinsed and patted dry
- 1 pound large shrimp, peeled and deveined
- 1 tablespoon olive oil
- 2 tablespoons unsalted butter
- 3 cloves garlic, minced
- 1/4 cup chopped fresh parsley
- 1/4 teaspoon paprika
- Salt and pepper to taste
- 1 cup low-sodium chicken broth
- 1/2 cup half-and-half or whole milk
- 2 tablespoons all-purpose flour
- 1/4 cup grated Parmesan cheese
- ·/4 cup breadcrumbs
- Lemon wedges for serving
- Fresh parsley for garnish

Steps for Cooking:

1. Preheat your oven to 375°F (190°C). Lightly grease a baking dish with olive oil.
2. Melt the butter in a skillet over medium heat and add minced garlic. Sauté for 1-2 minutes until fragrant.
3. Add the scallops and shrimp to the skillet. Sprinkle with chopped parsley, paprika, salt, and pepper. Cook for 2-3 minutes, stirring gently, until the seafood is slightly cooked.
4. In a separate bowl, whisk together chicken broth, half-and-half (or milk), and flour until smooth. Pour this mixture into the skillet with the seafood, stirring constantly until the sauce thickens, about 2-3 minutes. Remove from heat.
5. Transfer the seafood mixture to the prepared baking dish. Sprinkle grated Parmesan cheese evenly over the top, followed by breadcrumbs.
6. Bake in the oven for 15-20 minutes or until the crust turns golden brow and the seafood is cooked.
7. Remove from the oven and let it rest for a few minutes. Garnish with fresh parsley and serve with lemon wedges on the side.

1 serving approximately:
30g protein 10g carbs
12g fat 130mg cholesterol
400mg sodium 450mg potassium

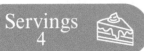 Servings 4

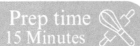 Prep time 15 Minutes

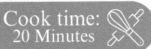 Cook time: 20 Minutes

Calories 280

Citrus Cod Fillet

Ingredients:

- 4 cod fillets (about 6 ounces each)
- 1 tablespoon olive oil
- 1 celery stalk, finely chopped
- 1 yellow bell pepper, diced
- Zest of 1 orange
- 2 tablespoons fresh orange juice
- Salt and pepper to taste
- Fresh parsley for garnish

Steps for Cooking:

1. Preheat your oven to 375°F (190°C). Lightly grease a baking dish with olive oil.
2. In a skillet, heat olive oil over medium heat. Add chopped celery and diced bell pepper. Sauté for about 3-4 minutes until slightly softened.
3. Place the cod fillets in the prepared baking dish. Season with salt and pepper.
4. Spoon the sautéed celery and capsicum mixture over the cod fillets.

5. Sprinkle the orange zest evenly over the fillets and drizzle with fresh orange juice.
6. Cover the baking dish with foil and bake in the preheated oven for 15-20 minutes or until the fish is cooked through and flakes easily with a fork.
7. Remove from the oven and let it rest for a few minutes. Garnish with fresh parsley before serving.

1 serving approximately:
30g protein 5g carbs
7g fat 60mg cholesterol
300mg sodium 500mg potassium

Servings	Prep time 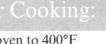	Cook time:	Calories
4	15 Minutes	20 Minutes	200

Salmon Steak with Vegetables

1 serving approximately:
30g protein 30g carbs
16g fat 75mg cholesterol
420mg sodium 850mg potassium

Ingredients:

- 4 salmon fish steaks (about 6 ounces each)
- 4 medium potatoes, washed and sliced
- 1 large onion, sliced
- 2 cups cherry tomatoes, halved
- 3 tablespoons olive oil
- Salt and pepper to taste
- 2 tablespoons chopped fresh parsley (optional, for garnish)

Steps for Cooking:

1. Preheat your oven to 400°F (200°C).
2. Line a large baking sheet with parchment paper.
3. Arrange the sliced potatoes, onion, and cherry tomatoes in a single layer on the prepared baking sheet.
4. Drizzle the vegetables with olive oil and season with salt and pepper. Toss gently to coat evenly.
5. Place the salmon steaks on top of the vegetables on the baking sheet.

6. Drizzle olive oil over the salmon steaks and season them with salt and pepper.
7. Bake in the preheated oven for about 20-25 minutes or until the salmon is cooked through, flakes easily with a fork, and the vegetables are tender.
8. Remove from the oven and garnish with chopped fresh parsley if desired.

Servings	Prep time 	Cook time:	Calories
4	15 Minutes	25 Minutes	370

Grilled Shrimp Skewers

Ingredients:

- 1 lb large shrimp, peeled and deveined
- 1 cup pineapple chunks
- 1 red bell pepper, cut into chunks
- 1 yellow bell pepper, cut into chunks
- 2 tbsp olive oil
- 2 tbsp fresh lime juice
- 1 tsp honey or maple syrup
- 1 tsp paprika
- Salt and pepper to taste
- Wooden skewers, soaked in water for 30 minutes

Steps for Cooking:

1. To create the marinade, whisk together olive oil, fresh lime juice, honey or maple syrup, paprika, salt, and pepper in a bowl.
2. Thread shrimp, pineapple, and bell pepper chunks alternately onto the soaked wooden skewers.
3. Place the skewers in a shallow dish and pour the marinade over them, coating them well. Marinate for at least 15 minutes.
4. Preheat a grill or grill pan over medium-high heat. Grill the shrimp skewers for 3-4 minutes per side or until they are pink and cooked through.
5. Serve the grilled shrimp skewers hot with additional lime wedges for squeezing over the top.

1 serving approximately:
25g protein 15g carbs
10g fat 160mg cholesterol
300mg sodium 500mg potassium

 Servings 4

 Prep time 15 Minutes

 Cook time: 10 Minutes

 Calories 250

---

1 serving approximately:
30g protein 12g carbs
12g fat 80mg cholesterol
350mg sodium 700mg potassium

Baked Seabass

Ingredients:

- 1 whole seabass (about 2 pounds), scaled, gutted, and cleaned, with the head removed
- 1 cup cherry tomatoes, halved
- 1 red onion, sliced
- 2 tablespoons olive oil
- 2 sprigs fresh rosemary
- Salt and pepper to taste
- Lemon wedges for serving
- Fresh parsley for garnish

Steps for Cooking:

1. Preheat your oven to 400°F (200°C). Line a baking sheet with parchment paper.
2. Rinse the seabass under cold water and pat dry with paper towels. Make sure it's spotless inside and out.
3. Place the seabass on the prepared baking sheet. Season the cavity and exterior generously with salt and pepper. Toss the cherry tomatoes and sliced red onion with olive oil, salt, and pepper in a bowl.

4. Stuff the cavity of the seabass with some of the tomato and onion mixture. Place the remaining vegetables around the fish on the baking sheet. Lay the fresh rosemary sprigs on top of the fish and around the vegetables.
5. Drizzle a bit more olive oil over the fish and vegetables. Bake in the preheated oven for about 20-25 minutes or until the fish is cooked and flakes easily with a fork.
6. Remove from the oven and let it rest for a few minutes before serving. Garnish with fresh parsley and serve with lemon wedges on the side.

 Servings 4

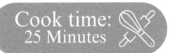 Prep time 15 Minutes

Cook time: 25 Minutes

 Calories 300

Baked Halibut

Ingredients:

- 1 pound halibut fillets, skinless
- 1 pint cherry tomatoes
- 1 lemon, thinly sliced
- 2 tablespoons olive oil
- 2 cloves garlic, minced
- 1 teaspoon dried rosemary
- Salt and pepper to taste
- Fresh parsley, chopped (optional, for garnish)

Steps for Cooking:

1. Preheat your oven to 400°F (200°C).
2. Place the halibut fillets in a large baking dish. Arrange cherry tomatoes and lemon slices around the fish.
3. Mix olive oil, minced garlic, dried rosemary, salt, and pepper in a small bowl.
4. Drizzle the olive oil mixture over the halibut, cherry tomatoes, and lemon slices, ensuring they are evenly coated.
5. Cover the baking dish with foil and bake in the oven for 15 minutes.
6. Remove the foil and continue baking for 5 minutes or until the fish is cooked and flakes easily with a fork.
7. Garnish with chopped fresh parsley before serving, if desired.

1 serving approximately:
28g protein 6g carbs
10g fat 60mg cholesterol
220mg sodium 600mg potassium

 Servings 4

 Prep time 10 Minutes

Cook time: 20 Minutes

Calories 230

Baked Stuffed Clams

1 serving approximately:
14g protein 10g carbs
9g fat 40mg cholesterol
350mg sodium 350mg potassium

Ingredients:

- 12 fresh clams, scrubbed and rinsed
- 1/2 cup whole-wheat breadcrumbs
- 2 tbsp chopped fresh parsley
- 2 tbsp chopped green onions
- 1 clove garlic, minced
- 1/4 cup grated Parmesan cheese
- 2 tbsp olive oil
- Lemon wedges for serving

Steps for Cooking:

1. Preheat the oven to 375°F (190°C). Place the scrubbed clams in a large pot with enough water to cover them. Bring to a boil over medium-high heat, then reduce heat to low and simmer for about 5 minutes or until the clams open. Remove from heat and let cool slightly.
2. Once cooled, carefully remove the clam meat from the shells and chop it finely. Set aside.

3. Combine whole-wheat breadcrumbs, chopped parsley, green onions, minced garlic, grated Parmesan cheese, olive oil, salt, and pepper in a bowl.
4. Mix well. Spoon the breadcrumb mixture onto each clam shell, pressing gently to form a mound.
5. Place the stuffed clams on a baking sheet lined with parchment paper. Bake in the oven for 15-20 minutes or until the breadcrumbs are golden brown and crispy. Serve the stuffed clams hot with lemon wedges for squeezing over the top.

Servings 4

Prep time 20 Minutes

Cook time: 20 Minutes

Calories 180

Creamy Shrimps

Ingredients:

- 1 pound large shrimp, peeled and deveined
- 2 tablespoons olive oil
- 3 cloves garlic, minced
- 1 onion, finely chopped
- 1 cup fresh spinach leaves, washed and chopped
- 1 cup low-sodium chicken broth
- 1 cup low-fat milk
- 2 tablespoons all-purpose flour
- Salt and pepper to taste
- Fresh parsley, chopped

Steps for Cooking:

1. In a large skillet, heat olive oil over medium heat. Add minced garlic and chopped onion, sauté until fragrant and onion is translucent.
2. Add the shrimp to the skillet and cook until they turn pink and opaque, about 2-3 minutes per side. Remove the shrimp from the skillet and set aside.
3. In the same skillet, add chopped spinach and cook until wilted, about 2 minutes.
4. Whisk together chicken broth, low-fat milk, and all-purpose flour until well combined in a small bowl. Pour the mixture into the skillet with spinach, stirring constantly until the sauce thickens, about 5 minutes.

1 serving approximately:
28g protein 12g carbs
14g fat 185mg cholesterol
360mg sodium 460mg potassium

5. Season the sauce with salt and pepper according to taste. Return the cooked shrimp to the skillet, stirring gently to coat the shrimp with the creamy sauce. Cook for 2-3 minutes until the shrimp are heated through. Garnish with chopped fresh parsley if desired before serving.

Servings	Prep time	Cook time:	Calories
4	15 Minutes	10 Minutes	250

Baked Mackerel Fish

1 serving approximately:
30g protein 2g carbs
14g fat 80mg cholesterol
100mg sodium 600mg potassium

Ingredients:

- 2 whole mackerel fish, about 1 pound each, cleaned and gutted
- 2 lemons, thinly sliced into rings
- 2 tablespoons olive oil
- 2 cloves garlic, minced
- 1 teaspoon paprika
- Salt and pepper to taste
- Fresh parsley, chopped

Steps for Cooking:

1. Preheat your oven to 400°F (200°C). Line a baking sheet with parchment paper or aluminum foil.
2. Make several diagonal incisions on both sides of each mackerel fish.
3. Insert lemon slices into the incisions on both sides of the fish.
4. Mix olive oil, minced garlic, paprika, salt and pepper in a small bowl.
5. Brush the olive oil mixture over the mackerel fish, ensuring they are evenly coated.

6. Place the fish on the prepared baking sheet and bake in the preheated oven for 20-25 minutes, or until it is cooked and flakes easily with a fork.
7. Garnish with chopped fresh parsley before serving, if desired.

Servings 	Prep time 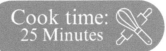	Cook time:	Calories
4	10 Minutes	25 Minutes	250

Pasta Farfalle with Seafood

Ingredients:

- 8 oz whole wheat farfalle pasta
- 2 tablespoons olive oil
- 2 cloves garlic, minced
- 1/2 pound octopus, cleaned and cut into bite-sized pieces
- 1/2 pound large shrimp, peeled and deveined
- 1/2 pound squid, cleaned and sliced into rings
- 1/2 pound scallops
- 1/2 pound mussels, scrubbed and debearded
- 1/4 teaspoon red pepper flakes (optional)
- 1 cup low-sodium vegetable broth
- 1/2 cup white wine (optional, can be replaced with more broth)
- 1 cup cherry tomatoes, halved
- 1/4 cup fresh parsley, chopped
- Salt and black pepper to taste
- Lemon wedges for serving

Steps for Cooking:

1. Cook the whole wheat farfalle pasta according to package instructions until al dente. Drain and set aside.
2. In a large skillet, heat the olive oil over medium heat. Add the garlic and sauté until fragrant, about 1 minute.
3. Add the octopus, shrimp, squid, and scallops to the skillet. Cook for 3-4 minutes, until the seafood starts to turn opaque.
4. Add the mussels, red pepper flakes, vegetable broth, and white wine (if using). Cover and cook for 5-7 minutes, until the mussels open and the seafood is cooked through. Discard any mussels that do not open.
5. Add the cooked pasta, cherry tomatoes, and parsley to the skillet. Toss to combine and cook for an additional 2-3 minutes, until heated through. Season with salt and black pepper to taste. Serve with lemon wedges.

1 serving approximately:
30g protein 45g carbs
10g fat 70mg cholesterol
400mg sodium 600mg potassium

 Servings 4

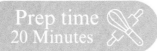 Prep time 20 Minutes

Cook time: 25 Minutes

 Calories 350

1 serving approximately:
3g protein 30g carbs
8g fat 5mg cholesterol
150mg sodium 500mg potassium

Sweet Potato Fries with Garlic Aioli

Ingredients:

- 2 large sweet potatoes, peeled and cut into fries
- 2 tablespoons olive oil
- 1/2 teaspoon paprika
- 1/2 teaspoon garlic powder
- Salt and pepper to taste
- Fresh parsley for garnish (optional)

For Garlic Aioli:

- 1/2 cup plain Greek yogurt
- 2 cloves garlic, minced
- 1 tablespoon lemon juice
- Salt and pepper to taste

Steps for Cooking:

1. Preheat your oven to 425°F (220°C) and line a baking sheet with parchment paper.
2. Toss the sweet potato fries in a large bowl with olive oil, paprika, garlic powder, salt, and pepper until evenly coated.
3. Spread the seasoned sweet potato fries in a single layer on the prepared baking sheet.
4. Bake in the preheated oven for 20-25 minutes, flipping halfway through, until the fries are golden brown and crispy.
5. While the fries are baking, prepare the garlic aioli. Combine the Greek yogurt, minced garlic, lemon juice, salt, and pepper in a small bowl. Mix well until smooth and creamy.
6. Remove the baked sweet potato fries from the oven and let them cool slightly.
7. Serve the baked sweet potato fries hot, garnished with fresh parsley if desired, and accompanied by the garlic aioli for dipping.

Servings 4

Prep time 15 Minutes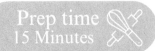

Cook time: 25 Minutes

Calories 200

Hummus

Ingredients:

- 1 (15-ounce) can chickpeas, drained and rinsed
- 1/4 cup tahini
- 2 tablespoons extra virgin olive oil
- 1 clove garlic, minced
- 3 tablespoons fresh lemon juice
- 1/2 teaspoon ground cumin
- 1/2 teaspoon salt
- 2-4 tablespoons water (as needed for desired consistency)
- pomegranate seeds
- chopped parsley

Steps for Cooking:

1. In a food processor, combine the chickpeas, tahini, olive oil, garlic, lemon juice, cumin, and salt. Process until smooth, adding water as needed to achieve desired consistency.
2. Taste and adjust seasoning with additional salt, lemon juice, or cumin if desired.
3. Transfer the hummus to a serving bowl. Garnish with whole chickpeas, pomegranate seeds, a drizzle of olive oil, and chopped parsley. Serve with whole grain pita bread or fresh vegetables.

1 serving approximately:
5g protein 14g carbs
12g fat 0mg cholesterol
2300mg sodium 160mg potassium

 Servings 4

Prep time 10 Minutes

Cook time: 0 Minutes

Calories 180

Egg and Cheese Muffins

1 serving approximately:
10g protein 2g carbs
8g fat 190mg cholesterol
320mg sodium 120mg potassium

Ingredients:

- 6 large eggs
- 1 cup low-fat cottage cheese
- 1/2 cup grated low-fat cheddar cheese
- 1/2 cup chopped spinach
- 1/4 cup chopped green onions
- 1/2 teaspoon salt
- 1/4 teaspoon black pepper
- 1 tablespoon fresh parsley, chopped (for garnish)
- 1 tablespoon sesame seeds (for garnish)

Steps for Cooking:

1. Preheat your oven to 350°F (175°C) and lightly grease a muffin tin or line it with paper muffin cups.
2. In a large bowl, whisk the eggs until well beaten. Add the cottage cheese, cheddar cheese, chopped spinach, green onions, salt, and black pepper. Mix until well combined.
3. Pour the mixture evenly into the prepared muffin tin, filling each cup about 3/4 full.
4. Bake in the preheated oven for 20 minutes, or until the muffins are set and lightly golden on top.
5. Remove from the oven and let cool slightly. Sprinkle with fresh parsley and sesame seeds before serving.

Servings 6

Prep time 10 Minutes

Cook time: 20 Minutes

Calories 120

Guacamole Sandwich

Ingredients:

- 4 slices of rice bread
- 1 large ripe avocado
- 1 tablespoon lime juice
- 1/4 teaspoon salt
- 1/4 teaspoon black pepper
- 1 medium tomato, thinly sliced
- Fresh basil leaves for decoration

1 serving approximately:
6g protein 38g carbs
17g fat 0mg cholesterol
360mg sodium 580mg potassium

Steps for Cooking:

1. Mash the ripe avocado with lime juice, salt, and black pepper in a bowl to make guacamole.
2. Toast the rice bread slices until lightly crispy.
3. Spread the guacamole evenly on two slices of the toasted rice bread.
4. Place the thinly sliced tomato on top of the guacamole.
5. Cover each sandwich with the remaining two slices of toasted rice bread.
6. Garnish with fresh basil leaves for decoration.
7. Serve the sandwiches immediately or wrap them in parchment paper for later consumption.

| Servings 2 | Prep time 15 Minutes | Cook time: 0 Minutes | Calories 320 |

1 serving approximately:
30g protein 4g carbs
1g fat 70mg cholesterol
500mg sodium 280mg potassium

Healthy Dry Turkey Jerky

Ingredients:

- 1 pound turkey breast, thinly sliced
- 1/4 cup low-sodium soy sauce
- 2 tablespoons Worcestershire sauce
- 1 tablespoon honey
- 1 teaspoon garlic powder
- 1/2 teaspoon onion powder
- 1/2 teaspoon black pepper
- Cooking spray

Steps for Cooking:

1. Combine the low-sodium soy sauce, Worcestershire sauce, honey, garlic powder, onion powder, and black pepper in a bowl. Mix well to make the marinade.
2. Add the thinly sliced turkey breast to the marinade, ensuring each slice is coated evenly. Cover the bowl and refrigerate for at least 4 hours or overnight for the best flavor.
3. Preheat your oven to 175°F (80°C) and line a baking sheet with parchment paper. Place a wire rack on top of the baking sheet.
4. Remove the marinated turkey slices from the bowl and pat them dry with paper towels. Place the slices on the wire rack, leaving space between each slice for air circulation.

5. Bake the turkey slices in the preheated oven for about 3 hours or until they are dried and firm but still pliable. Check occasionally and flip the slices halfway through the cooking time. Once the turkey jerky is done, remove it from the oven and let it cool completely. Store the jerky in an airtight container at room temperature for up to 2 weeks.

| Servings 4 | Prep time 15 Minutes | Cook time: 3 hours | Calories 150 |

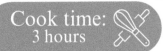

Shrimp Spring Rolls

Ingredients:

- 8 large shrimp, peeled and deveined
- 4 rice paper wrappers
- 1 cup shredded lettuce
- 1 cup shredded carrots
- 1/2 cucumber, julienned
- 2 green onions, cut into thin strips (feathers)
- Fresh cilantro leaves
- Fresh mint leaves
- 2 tablespoons low-sodium soy sauce
- 1 tablespoon rice vinegar
- 1 teaspoon honey
- 1/2 teaspoon grated ginger
- 1/2 teaspoon minced garlic
- 1/4 teaspoon red pepper flakes (optional)
- Water for soaking rice paper wrappers

Steps for Cooking:

1. To create the dipping sauce, mix soy sauce, rice vinegar, honey, grated ginger, minced garlic, and red pepper flakes (if using) in a bowl. Set aside.
2. Preheat a grill pan or skillet over medium heat. Grill the shrimp for 2-3 minutes per side until cooked through. Remove from heat and let them cool slightly.
3. Prepare a large bowl of warm water. Dip one rice paper wrapper into the water for 5-10 seconds until it becomes soft and pliable.
4. Lay the softened rice paper on a clean surface. On the bottom third of the wrapper, place a few shredded lettuce leaves, carrots, cucumber, cilantro leaves, mint leaves, green onion feathers, and one grilled shrimp.
5. Fold the sides of the wrapper over the filling, then roll tightly from the bottom up to form a spring roll.
6. Repeat the process with the remaining wrappers and filling ingredients.
7. Serve the shrimp spring rolls with the prepared dipping sauce on the side.

1 serving approximately:
10g protein 20g carbs
4g fat 45mg cholesterol
250mg sodium 230mg potassium

 Servings 4

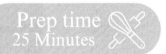 **Prep time** 25 Minutes

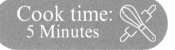 **Cook time:** 5 Minutes

 Calories 160

Slices of Apples with Peanut Butter

1 serving approximately:
3g protein 19g carbs
8g fat 0mg cholesterol
60mg sodium 200mg potassium

Ingredients:

- 2 medium-sized apples
- 1/4 cup natural peanut butter (unsweetened)
- 1 tablespoon honey (optional)
- 1/4 teaspoon ground cinnamon (optional)
- Chopped nuts or seeds for garnish (optional)

Steps for Cooking:

1. Wash the apples thoroughly and pat them dry. Cut each apple into thin slices.
2. In a small bowl, mix the natural peanut butter with honey and ground cinnamon (if using) until well combined.
3. Spread a thin layer of the peanut butter mixture onto each apple slice.
4. Arrange the peanut butter-coated apple slices on a serving plate.
5. Optionally, sprinkle chopped nuts or seeds over the top for added crunch and nutrition.

 Servings 4

 **Prep time** 10 Minutes

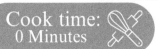 **Cook time:** 0 Minutes

 Calories 150

Caprese Skewers

Ingredients:

- 1 pint cherry tomatoes
- 8 ounces fresh mozzarella cheese, cut into bite-sized cubes
- Fresh basil leaves
- Balsamic glaze (store-bought or homemade)
- Wooden skewers

1 serving approximately:
8g protein 5g carbs
7g fat 25mg cholesterol
100mg sodium 150mg potassium

Steps for Cooking:

1. Rinse the cherry tomatoes and pat them dry with paper towels. Rinse the fresh basil leaves as well and pat them dry.
2. Assemble the skewers by threading one cherry tomato, one cube of mozzarella cheese, and one basil leaf onto each skewer. Repeat this process until all ingredients are used, making about 12 skewers.
3. Arrange the assembled skewers on a serving platter.
4. Drizzle balsamic glaze over the skewers just before serving. You can also serve extra glaze on the side for dipping.

Servings 4	Prep time 15 Minutes	Cook time: 0 Minutes	Calories 120

Eggs Stuffed with Herring Creamy Pate

1 serving approximately:
12g protein 4g carbs
13g fat 245mg cholesterol
320mg sodium 210mg potassium

Ingredients:

- 4 hard-boiled eggs, peeled and halved lengthwise
- 1/2 cup herring creamy pate
- 2 tablespoons Greek yogurt (plain, low-fat)
- 1 teaspoon Dijon mustard
- 1 tablespoon fresh dill, chopped
- Salt and black pepper to taste
- Dill sprigs for garnish

Steps for Cooking:

1. Remove the yolks from the halved hard-boiled eggs and place them in a mixing bowl.
2. Add herring creamy pate, Greek yogurt, Dijon mustard, chopped fresh dill, salt, and black pepper to the bowl with the egg yolks. Mix until well combined and creamy.
3. Spoon the herring creamy pate mixture into the hollowed-out egg whites, filling them evenly.
4. Arrange the stuffed eggs on a serving platter and garnish each egg with a small dill sprig on top.

Servings 4	Prep time 15 Minutes	Cook time: 0 Minutes	Calories 180

1 serving approximately:
6g protein 15g carbs
3g fat 5mg cholesterol
30mg sodium 150mg potassium

Raspberry Yogurt Jelly Cake

Ingredients:

- 1 packet unflavored gelatin (about 7g)
- 1/4 cup cold water
- 1 cup plain Greek yogurt
- 2 tablespoons honey or maple syrup
- 1 teaspoon vanilla extract
- 1 cup fresh raspberries
- 2 tablespoons dried raspberries
- Fresh rosemary leaves and dry flowers for garnish

Steps for Cooking:

1. In a small bowl, sprinkle the gelatin over cold water and let it soften for 5 minutes.
2. Heat the gelatin mixture in a saucepan over low heat until completely dissolved, stirring constantly. Remove from heat and let it cool slightly.
3. Combine Greek yogurt, honey or maple syrup, and vanilla extract in a mixing bowl. Mix well.
4. Add the cooled gelatin mixture to the yogurt mixture and stir until smooth and well combined.
5. Gently fold the fresh raspberries into the yogurt-gelatin mixture.
6. Place the dried raspberries in a circle around the bottom of a round silicone mold.
7. Pour the yogurt-gelatin mixture into the mold over the dried raspberries, smoothing the top with a spatula.
8. Place the mold in the freezer and let it freeze for at least 2 hours or until set.
9. Once set, remove the jelly cake from the mold and transfer it to a serving plate.
10. Garnish with some dried raspberries, fresh berries, rosemary, and dry flowers if desired.

Servings 4

Prep time 20 Minutes

Cook time: 2 hours

Calories 110

Chocolate Banana Brownies

1 serving approximately:
2g protein 20g carbs
3g fat 0mg cholesterol
90mg sodium 150mg potassium

Ingredients:

- 2 ripe bananas, mashed
- 1/2 cup unsweetened applesauce
- 1/4 cup honey or maple syrup
- 1/4 cup unsweetened cocoa powder
- 1/4 cup whole wheat flour
- 1/4 cup almond flour
- 1 teaspoon baking powder
- 1/4 teaspoon salt
- 1/4 cup dark chocolate chips (optional)
- Chopped walnuts or pecans for topping (optional)

Steps for Cooking:

1. Preheat your oven to 350°F (175°C) and grease an 8x8 inch baking dish.
2. Combine the mashed bananas, applesauce, honey or maple syrup, and cocoa powder in a large mixing bowl. Mix until well combined.
3. Add the whole wheat flour, almond flour, baking powder, and salt to the banana mixture. Stir until just combined. If using, fold in the dark chocolate chips.
4. Pour the batter into the prepared baking dish and spread it evenly with a spatula. If desired, sprinkle chopped walnuts or pecans on top.
5. Bake in the oven for about 25 minutes or until a toothpick inserted into the center comes clean.

6. Allow the brownies to cool in the pan for 10 minutes, then transfer them to a wire rack to cool completely before slicing them into squares.

Servings	Prep time 	Cook time:	Calories
12	15 Minutes	25 Minutes	110

1 serving approximately:
7g protein 30g carbs
8g fat 0mg cholesterol
60mg sodium 300mg potassium

Peach Chia Dessert

Ingredients:

- 1 cup plain Greek yogurt
- 1/2 cup chia seeds
- 2 ripe peaches, peeled and sliced
- 1 cup fresh blueberries
- 2 tablespoons honey (optional)
- Fresh mint leaves, for garnish

Steps for Cooking:

1. In a bowl, mix the Greek yogurt and chia seeds until well combined. Let it sit for 10-15 minutes to let the chia seeds absorb some yogurt and thicken.
2. In a blender, puree one peach until smooth. If desired, add honey to sweeten the puree.
3. To assemble the dessert glasses, spoon a layer of the chia seed yogurt mixture into the bottom of each glass.
4. Next, pour a layer of the peach puree over the chia seed yogurt layer.
5. Top the peach puree with fresh blueberries and a few slices of fresh peach.
6. Garnish each glass with fresh mint leaves.

Servings	Prep time 	Cook time:	Calories
4	15 Minutes	0 Minutes	220

Carrot Cake with Yogurt Cream

Ingredients:

- 1 1/2 cups whole wheat flour
- 1 teaspoon baking powder
- 1/2 teaspoon baking soda
- 1/2 teaspoon ground cinnamon
- 1/4 teaspoon ground nutmeg
- 1/4 teaspoon ground ginger
- Pinch of salt
- 1/2 cup unsweetened applesauce
- 1/2 cup maple syrup
- 1/4 cup olive oil
- 2 eggs
- 1 teaspoon vanilla extract
- 1/2 cups grated carrots
- 1/2 cup chopped walnuts or pecans
- Cooking spray

For the Yogurt Cream:
- 1 cup plain Greek yogurt
- 2 tablespoons honey
- 1 teaspoon vanilla extract

For Serving:
- Date syrup
- Mango puree (optional)
- Small edible flowers for garnish

Steps for Cooking:

1. Preheat your oven to 350°F (175°C). Grease and flour two round cake pans.
2. Whisk together the whole wheat flour, baking powder, baking soda, cinnamon, nutmeg, ginger, and salt
 in a medium bowl.
3. Mix the applesauce, maple syrup, olive oil, eggs, and vanilla extract in another bowl until well combined.
4. Gradually add the wet ingredients to the dry ingredients, stirring until combined. Fold in the grated carrots and chopped nuts.
5. Divide the batter evenly between the prepared cake pans. Bake in the preheated oven for about 25-30 minutes or until a toothpick inserted into the center comes out clean.
6. Allow the cakes to cool in the pans for 10 minutes before transferring them to a wire rack to cool completely.

For the Yogurt Cream:
1. Combine Greek yogurt, honey, and vanilla extract in a bowl. Mix until smooth and creamy.

Assembly:
1. Once the cakes have cooled completely, spread a layer of yogurt cream on top of one cake layer.
2. Place the second cake layer on top and spread the remaining yogurt cream on top of the cake.
3. Decorate the cake with pieces of nuts and tiny edible flowers.
4. Optional: Make dots of mango puree on the cake for added flavor and presentation.
5. Drizzle date syrup over the cake just before serving.

Servings	Prep time	Cook time:	Calories
4	15 Minutes	20 Minutes	280

1 serving approximately:
6g protein 38g carbs
12g fat 45mg cholesterol
180mg sodium 300mg potassium

Meringue Cake Pavlova

1 serving approximately:
2g protein 42g carbs
5g fat 10mg cholesterol
550mg sodium 220mg potassium

Ingredients:

- 3 large egg whites at room temperature
- 3/4 cup granulated sugar
- 1 teaspoon cornstarch
- 1 teaspoon white vinegar
- 1/2 teaspoon vanilla extract
- 1 cup fresh mango, diced
- 2 passion fruits, pulp scooped out
- 1 cup low-fat whipped cream

Steps for Cooking:

1. Preheat your oven to 250°F (120°C). Line a baking sheet with parchment paper.
2. In a clean, dry mixing bowl, beat the egg whi tes quickly until soft peaks form.
3. Gradually add the granulated sugar, one tablespoon at a time, while beating until stiff peaks form and the meringue is glossy.
4. Gently fold in the cornstarch, white vinegar, and vanilla extract into the meringue until well combined.
5. Spoon the meringue onto the prepared baking sheet, forming a circle or oval shape to create the Pavlova base.
6. Use the back of a spoon to create a well in the center of the meringue base, leaving a slight rim around the edges.

7. Bake the meringue in the oven for about 1 hour or until the outside is crisp and dry. Turn off the oven and let the meringue cool completely inside the oven with the door slightly open.
8. Once cooled, transfer the meringue to a serving plate. Spread the whipped cream evenly over the meringue base.
9. Arrange the diced fresh mango and passion fruit pulp on the whipped cream.

| Servings 4  | Prep time 20 Minutes 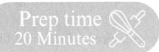 | Cook time: 1 hour | Calories 215 |

Vanilla Puddings

1 serving approximately:
2g protein 30g carbs
4g fat 0mg cholesterol
80mg sodium 200mg potassium

Ingredients:

- 2 cups almond milk
- 1/4 cup cornstarch
- 1/4 cup maple syrup or agave nectar
- 1 teaspoon vanilla extract
- Fresh blackberries, for serving
- Date syrup, for serving

Steps for Cooking:

1. Whisk 1/4 cup almond milk and cornstarch in a small bowl until smooth and no lumps remain.
2. Combine the remaining almond milk, maple syru or agave nectar, and vanilla extract in a saucepan. Heat over medium heat until it starts to simmer.
3. Slowly pour the cornstarch mixture into the simmering almond milk while whisking continuousl to prevent lumps.
4. Continue to cook and whisk until the mixture thickens to a pudding-like consistency, about 5-7 minutes. Remove the pudding from heat and let it cool slightly.

5. Divide the pudding into serving cups or ramekins. Cover each pudding cup with plastic wrap, ensuring the wrap touches the surface of the pudding to prevent skin from forming. Refrigerate the puddings for at least 2 hours or until chilled and set. When ready to serve, top each pudding with fresh blackberries and a drizzle of date syrup.

| Servings 4 | Prep time 10 Minutes  | Cook time: 10 Minutes 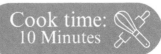 | Calories 160 |

Baked Cheesecake

Ingredients:

- 1 1/2 cups graham cracker crumbs
- 1/4 cup unsalted butter, melted
- 16 oz low-fat cream cheese, softened
- 1/2 cup plain Greek yogurt
- 1/2 cup honey or maple syrup
- 2 large eggs
- 1 teaspoon vanilla extract
- 1/2 cup fresh raspberries
- Fresh mint leaves and raspberries for garnish

Steps for Cooking:

1. Preheat your oven to 325°F (163°C). Grease a 9-inch round baking pan with cooking spray.
2. In a mixing bowl, combine the graham cracker crumbs and melted butter. Press the mixture evenly onto the bottom of the prepared baking pan.
3. In another bowl, beat the cream cheese, Greek yogurt, honey or maple syrup, eggs, and vanilla extract until smooth and creamy.
4. Gently fold the fresh raspberries into the cream cheese mixture.
5. Pour the cream cheese mixture over the graham cracker crust in the baking pan, spreading it evenly.
6. Bake in the oven for about 50 minutes or until the cheesecake is set and the edges are lightly golden.
7. Remove from the oven and let it cool completely at room temperature. Once cooled, refrigerate the cheesecake for at least 2 hours or until chilled and firm. Garnish with fresh mint leaves and raspberries before serving.

1 serving approximately:
9g protein 25g carbs
21g fat 80mg cholesterol
200mg sodium 180mg potassium

 Servings 6

 **Prep time** 20 Minutes

Cook time: 50 Minutes

 Calories 320

Creamy Matcha Ice Cream

1 serving approximately:
2g protein 35g carbs
1g fat 0mg cholesterol
1mg sodium 500mg potassium

Ingredients:

- 4 ripe bananas, peeled, sliced, and frozen
- 2 tablespoons matcha green tea powder
- 1/4 teaspoon vanilla extract
- Fresh mint leaves, chopped (for garnish)

Steps for Cooking:

1. In a food processor or blender, combine the frozen banana slices, matcha green tea powder, and vanilla extract.
2. Blend the ingredients until smooth and creamy, scraping down the sides of the processor or blender as needed.
3. Transfer the matcha banana mixture to a freezer-safe container. Cover and freeze for at least 4 hours or until firm.
4. Once frozen, scoop the Heart-Healthy Creamy Matcha Ice Cream with Frozen Banana into bowls or cones.
5. Garnish with chopped fresh mint leaves for added flavor and freshness.

 **Servings** 4

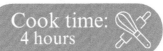 **Prep time** 10 Minutes

Cook time: 4 hours

  Calories 150

Banana Muffins

Ingredients:

- 1 1/2 cups whole wheat flour
- 1 teaspoon baking powder
- 1/2 teaspoon baking soda
- 1/4 teaspoon salt
- 3 ripe bananas, mashed
- 1/2 cup unsweetened applesauce
- 1/4 cup honey or maple syrup
- 1/4 cup almond milk (unsweetened)
- 1/4 cup coconut oil, melted
- 1 teaspoon vanilla extract
- 1/2 cup flaked almond nuts, plus extra for topping
- Cooking spray

Steps for Cooking:

1. Preheat your oven to 350°F (175°C). Line a muffin tin with paper liners and lightly coat them with cooking spray.
2. Whisk together the whole wheat flour, baking powder, baking soda, and salt
3. In a large mixing bowl.
4. Combine the mashed bananas, unsweetened applesauce, honey or maple syrup, almond milk, melted coconut oil, and vanilla extract in another bowl. Mix well.
5. Add the wet ingredients to the dry ingredients and stir until just combined. Fold in the flaked almond nuts.
6. Divide the batter evenly among the prepared muffin cups, filling each about three-quarters full.
7. Top each muffin with a sprinkle of flaked almond nuts.

8. Bake in the oven for 18-20 minutes or until a toothpick inserted into the center comes clean. Remove from the oven and let the muffins cool in the pan for 5 minutes before transferring them to a wire rack to cool completely.

1 serving approximately:
3g protein 24g carbs
6g fat 0mg cholesterol
120mg sodium 200mg potassium

 Servings 4

 Prep time 15 Minutes

 Cook time: 20 Minutes

 Calories 160

---

1 serving approximately:
2g protein 35g carbs
6g fat 0mg cholesterol
5mg sodium 220mg potassium

Baked Apples

Ingredients:

- 4 medium apples (such as Honeycrisp or Granny Smith)
- 1/4 cup almond flakes
- 1/4 cup chopped almonds
- 2 tablespoons honey
- 1/4 cup raisins
- 1/4 cup fresh orange juice
- 1 teaspoon ground cinnamon
- 4 star anise for garnish

Steps for Cooking:

1. Preheat your oven to 350°F (175°C).
2. Core the apples, removing the seeds and creating a cavity for the filling.
3. In a small bowl, mix together the almond flakes, chopped almonds, honey, raisins, orange juice, and ground cinnamon.
4. Fill each apple with the prepared mixture Place the stuffed apples in a baking dish.
5. Pour a little water into the bottom of the dish to prevent the apples from drying out.
6. Bake in the preheated oven for 30 minutes, or until the apples are tender.

7. Remove the baked apples from the oven and let them cool slightly. Garnish each apple with a star anise before serving.

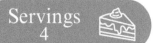 Servings 4

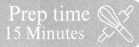 Prep time 15 Minutes

 Cook time: 30 Minutes

 Calories 180

Blueberry Scones

Ingredients:

- 1 cup whole wheat flour
- 1 cup all-purpose flour
- 1/4 cup granulated sugar
- 1 tablespoon baking powder
- 1/4 teaspoon salt
- 1/4 cup cold unsalted butter
- 3/4 cup low-fat buttermilk
- 1 large egg
- 1 teaspoon vanilla extract
- ·1 cup fresh or frozen blueberries
- 1/2 cup powdered sugar
- 1 tablespoon lemon juice
- 1 teaspoon lemon zest

Steps for Cooking:

1. Preheat your oven to 400°F (200°C) and line a baking sheet with parchment paper.
2. In a large bowl, whisk together the whole wheat flour, all-purpose flour, granulated sugar, baking powder, and salt. Cut in the cold butter using a pastry blender or your fingers until the mixture resembles coarse crumbs.
3. In a small bowl, whisk together the buttermilk, egg, and vanilla extract. Add the wet ingredients to the dry ingredients and stir until just combined. Gently fold in the blueberries.
4. Turn the dough out onto a lightly floured surface and knead gently until it comes together. Pat the dough into a 1-inch thick circle and cut into 6 wedges. Place the wedges on the prepared baking sheet and bake for 18-20 minutes
5. While the scones are baking, mix the powdered sugar, lemon juice, and lemon zest in a small bowl until smooth. Drizzle the glaze over the warm scones before serving.

1 serving approximately:
5g protein 30g carbs
8g fat 0mg cholesterol
60mg sodium 300mg potassium

Servings 6	Prep time 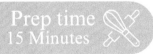 15 Minutes	Cook time:  20 Minutes	Calories 220

Coconut Date Balls

1 serving (1 ball) approximately:
3g protein 10g carbs
9g fat 0mg cholesterol
50mg sodium 100mg potassium

Ingredients:

- 1/2 cup almond butter
- 1/4 cup chopped nuts
- 1/4 cup chopped dried fruit
- 1/4 cup chopped dates
- 2 tablespoons ground flax seeds
- 2 tablespoons hemp seeds
- 2 tablespoons maple syrup
- teaspoon vanilla extract
- Pinch of salt
- 1/2 cup shredded coconut flakes

Steps for Cooking:

1. In a large mixing bowl, combine almond butter, chopped nuts, chopped dried fruit, chopped dates, ground flax seeds, hemp seeds, maple syrup or agave nectar, vanilla extract, and a pinch of salt.
2. Mix everything well until the mixture comes together and is evenly combined. Using clean hands, roll the mixture into small balls about 1 inch in diameter.
3. Place the shredded coconut flakes in a shallow bowl or plate. Roll each ball in the shredded coconut flakes until well coated, pressing gently to adhere the coconut. Place the coconut-dipped balls on a parchment-lined baking sheet. Once all the balls are coated and placed on the baking sheet, refrigerate them for about 30 minutes to firm up. After chilling, the coconut-dipped energy protein balls are ready to eat. Any leftovers can be stored in an airtight container in the refrigerator for up to one week.

Servings 12	Prep time  15 Minutes	Cook time:  0 minutes	Calories 130

Chapter 10: Sauce Recipes
Pesto Sauce

Ingredients:

- 2 cups fresh basil leaves, packed
- 1/4 cup pine nuts or walnuts
- 2 garlic cloves, minced
- 1/4 cup grated Parmesan cheese
- 1/2 cup extra virgin olive oil
- Salt and pepper to taste

Steps for Cooking:

1. Combine the fresh basil leaves, pine nuts or walnuts, minced garlic, and grated Parmesan cheese in a food processor.
2. Pulse the ingredients a few times to break them down.
3. With the food processor running, slowly drizzle in the extra virgin olive oil until the mixture forms a smooth paste.
4. Add salt and pepper to taste, and pulse a few more times to combine.
5. Taste the pesto sauce and adjust the seasoning if needed.
6. Transfer the pesto sauce to a jar or container with a tight-fitting lid.
7. Store the pesto sauce in the refrigerator for up to one week, or freeze it in ice cube trays for more extended storage.
8. Use pesto sauce as a flavorful topping for whole-grain pasta, grilled chicken or fish, roasted vegetables, or as a dip for whole-grain bread.

Tzatziki Cucumber Yogurt Sauce

Ingredients:

- 1 cup plain Greek yogurt (low-fat)
- 1 medium cucumber, peeled, seeded, and grated
- 2 cloves garlic, minced
- 1 tablespoon fresh lemon juice
- 1 tablespoon extra-virgin olive oil
- 1 tablespoon chopped fresh dill
- Salt and black pepper to taste

Steps for Cooking:

1. Combine the Greek yogurt, grated cucumber, minced garlic, fresh lemon juice, extra-virgin olive oil, and chopped fresh dill in a mixing bowl.
2. Season with salt and black pepper according to your taste preferences.
3. Stir all the ingredients together until well combined.
4. Cover the bowl and refrigerate the cucumber yogurt sauce for at least 30 minutes to allow the flavors to meld.
5. Before serving, stir the sauce a good bit. Garnish with additional fresh dill if desired.
6. Enjoy it as a refreshing dip or sauce for grilled meats, salads, or sandwiches.

Red Italian Marinara Sauce

Ingredients:

- 2 tablespoons extra virgin olive oil
- 1 small onion, finely chopped
- 2 cloves garlic, minced
- 1 can (28 ounces) crushed tomatoes
- 1 teaspoon dried oregano
- 1 teaspoon dried basil
- 1/2 teaspoon red pepper flakes (adjust to taste)
- Salt and black pepper to taste

Steps for Cooking:

1. In a saucepan, heat the extra virgin olive oil over medium heat.
2. Add the finely chopped onion and minced garlic to the pan. Cook occasionally until the onion is translucent and the garlic is fragrant, about 3-4 minutes.
3. Pour in the crushed tomatoes and stir to combine with the onion and garlic.
4. Add the dried oregano, dried basil, red pepper flakes, salt, and black pepper to the sauce. Stir well to incorporate the herbs and spices.
5. Bring the sauce to a simmer, then reduce the heat to low. Cover the saucepan and let the marinara sauce cook gently for about 20 minutes, stirring occasionally.
6. Taste the sauce and adjust the seasoning, adding more salt, pepper, or red pepper flakes according to your preferences.
7. Remove it from heat once the sauce has thickened and the flavors have melded together. Garnish with chopped fresh basil leaves if desired. Serve the Red Italian Marinara Sauce over whole grain pasta, zucchini noodles, or as a dipping sauce.

Conclusion

We have reached the end of our culinary journey through the world of heart-healthy recipes. Now, I would like to introduce you to the 60-Day Meal Plan. With this meal plan, you won't have to worry about what to make for breakfast, lunch, dinner, or snacks for the next 60 days. This plan is more than just a list of recipes from the book; it is a comprehensive guide that considers the caloric content and ensures the presence of all essential micro and macro nutrients. For convenience, each recipe name in the meal plan is accompanied by its corresponding page number.

Each day's meals are designed to total about 2000 calories, which is the average daily caloric intake for an adult. If you require more calories, you can increase portion sizes by eating one and a half or two servings of a dish per meal. Conversely, if you need fewer calories, you can reduce portion sizes or eliminate snacks.

This meal plan is ideal for two people. Simply follow the instructions, and you will have meals for every part of the day without leftovers or the need for extra cooking. If you have more family members, you can double or triple the portions for each recipe to ensure there is enough food for everyone, with no leftovers.

You may notice that some dishes in the meal plan repeat. This design is intentional to minimize cooking time while still providing balanced and nutritious meals daily. For instance, you might prepare a meat dish for lunch with four servings. You can have two servings for lunch and save the remaining two for dinner. In the evening, simply reheat the meat dish and add a salad or fresh vegetables.

I have a particular fondness for mid-morning and afternoon snacks. If you feel hungry between meals, you can prepare snacks in advance and take them to work or on a walk. If eating five times a day is inconvenient, you can combine the snacks with your main meals and stick to three meals a day.

I am passionate about cooking and love creating interesting, tasty, and healthy recipes. I have put all my knowledge about nutrition and heart health into this book, so you can enjoy easy and delicious meals for many years to come.

Meal Plan

Day	Breakfast	Mid-Morning Snack	Lunch	Afternoon Snack	Dinner
1	Whole Grain Pancakes (p.13)	Guacamole Sandwich (p.64)	Pomegranate Glazed Duck Breast (p. 41) & brown rice (5oz cooked) & fresh vegetables (7oz)	Peach Chia Dessert (p. 41)	Pomegranate Glazed Duck Breast (p. 68) & Quinoa Pilaf (p. 30)
2	Whole Grain Pancakes (p.13)	Peach Chia Dessert (p.41)	Filet Mignon (p.45) & Quinoa Pilaf (p.30)	Hazelnuts (up to 2oz)	Black Bean & Turkey Chili (p.43)
3	Salmon Quesadilla (p.20)	Grilled Halloumi and Rocket Salad (p.31)	Black Bean & Turkey Chili (p.43) & 2 slices of whole wheat bread & fresh vegetables (7oz)	Fresh blueberries or other berries (7oz)	Sesame Tuna Steaks (p.53) & Grilled Halloumi and Rocket Salad (p.31)
4	Steel-cut oats (p.18)	Cashew Nuts (1oz) and strawberries (5oz)	Fish Meatballs (p.53) & whole wheat spaghetti (5oz)	Banana Muffins (p.72)	Stuffed Potato Boats (p.49) & fresh vegetables (7oz)
5	Sweet Potatoes and Eggs (p.17)	Banana Muffins (p.72)	Quinoa Salad (p.33) & Stuffed Potato Boats (p.49) & 2 slices of whole wheat bread	Banana Muffins (p.72)	Baked Seabass (p.58) & Quinoa Salad (p.33)
6	Broccoli and Cheese Quiche (p.15)	Banana Muffins (p.72)	Pesto Pasta (p.26) & Baked Seabass (p.58)	1 apple	Mediterranean Style Cod (p.55) & Pesto Pasta (p.26)
7	Broccoli and Cheese Quiche (p.15)	Banana Muffins (p.72)	Buddha Bowl with Quinoa (p.23) & Mediterranean Style Cod (p.55) & 2 slices of whole wheat bread	Banana Muffins (p.72)	Stir Fry Noodles with Beef (p.50)
8	Turkey Sausage Skillet (p.19) & fresh berries (7oz)	Cashew nuts (1 oz.) and 1 orange	Cauliflower Rice Salad (p.34) & Stir Fry Noodles with Beef (p.50)	Slices of Apples with Peanut Butter (p.65)	Salmon Steak with Vegetables (p.57) & Cauliflower Rice Salad (p.34)
9	Turkey Sausage Skillet (p.19) & hazelnuts (1oz)	2 Coconut Date Balls (p.73)	Salmon Steak with Vegetables (p.57) & Greek Roasted Potatoes (p.26)	2 Coconut Date Balls (p.73)	Stuffed Chicken Breast (p.43) & Greek Roasted Potatoes (p.26)
10	Blueberry Smoothie Bowl (p.21)	2 Coconut Date Balls (p.73)	Stuffed Chicken Breast (p.43) & Stewed Bulgur (p.25)	1 apple	Baked Pork (p.45) & Stewed Bulgur (p.25) & fresh vegetables (7oz)
11	Mediterranean Omelette (p.17) & Baked Pork (p.45)	Baked Cheesecake (p.71)	Spicy Stir-Fry Shrimps (p.55) & brown rice (5oz cooked) & fresh vegetables (7oz)	Hazelnuts (up to 2oz)	Spicy Stir-Fry Shrimps (p.55) & Beet Salad with Orange (p.32)
12	Overnight Oats (p.20)	Baked Cheesecake (p.71)	Lamb Kabobs (p.48) & Beet Salad with Orange (p.32)	Baked Cheesecake (p.71)	Lamb Kabobs (p.48) & Grilled Vegetable Platter (p.30)
13	Creamy Yogurt Delight (p.14)	Fresh Salad (p.34)	Cauliflower Soup with Chicken Meatballs (p.13) & Coconut Chicken Curry (p.13) & 2 slices of whole wheat bread	Fresh Salad (p.13)	Coconut Chicken Curry (p.13) & Grilled Vegetable Platter (p.13)
14	Banana Casserole (p.13)	Guacamole Sandwich (p.13)	Cauliflower Soup with Chicken Meatballs (p.39) & Teriyaki Glazed Salmon (p.54)	Banana Casserole (p.21)	Teriyaki Glazed Salmon (p.54) & Lemon Herb Couscous (p.29)
15	Tuna and Mango Wrap (p.18)	1 cup Greek yogurt & fresh berries (5oz)	Thai Chicken Satay (p.50) & Lemon Herb Couscous (p.29)	Cashew nuts (1oz)	Thai Chicken Satay (p.50) & brown rice (5oz cooked)

Day	Breakfast	Mid-Morning Snack	Lunch	Afternoon Snack	Dinner
16	Stuffed Peppers (p.14)	Carrot Cake with Yogurt Cream (p.69)	Stuffed Peppers (p.14) & Chicken Thighs (p.46)	Carrot Cake with Yogurt Cream (p.69)	Chicken Thighs (p.46) & Quinoa Salad (p.33)
17	Veggie Muffins (p.22)	Carrot Cake with Yogurt Cream (p.69)	Stuffed Potato Boats (p.49) & Quinoa Salad (p.33)	Carrot Cake with Yogurt Cream (p.69)	Stuffed Potato Boats (p.49) & Roasted Cauliflower (p.28)
18	Veggie Muffins (p.22)	Hazelnuts (up to 2oz)	Creamy Mushroom Soup (p.38) & Lamb Burgers (p.51)	Healthy Dry Turkey Jerky (p.64)	Lamb Burgers (p.51) & Roasted Cauliflower (p.28)
19	Green Smoothie Bowl (p.15)	Creamy Mushroom Soup (p.38) & Pecans (1oz)	Eggplant Boats with Meat (p.44) & whole wheat spaghetti (5 oz cooked)	Healthy Dry Turkey Jerky (p.64)	Eggplant Boats with Meat (p.44) & 2 slices of whole wheat bread
20	Oatmeal with Chicken (p.22)	Raspberry Yogurt Jelly Cake (p.67) & Pecans (1oz)	Scallops and Shrimp Delight (p.56) & rice (7oz cooked) & fresh vegetables (7oz)	Guacamole Sandwich (p.64) & 1 apple	Scallops and Shrimp Delight (p.56) & fresh vegetables (7oz)
21	Oatmeal with Chicken (p.22)	Raspberry Yogurt Jelly Cake (p.67) & Pecans (1 oz.)	Stir Fry Noodles with Beef (p.50) & fresh vegetables (7oz)	Broccoli and Cheese Quiche (p.15)	Chicken Vegetable Bowl (p.32) & 2 slices of whole wheat bread
22	Broccoli and Cheese Quiche (p.15)	Meringue Cake Pavlova (p.70)	White Salmon Chowder (p.37) & 2 slices of whole wheat bread & Chicken Vegetable Bowl (p.32)	Meringue Cake Pavlova (p.70)	Baked Seabass (p.58) & fresh vegetables (7oz)
23	Sweet Potatoes and Eggs (p.17) & cashew nuts (1oz)	1 cup Greek yogurt & fresh berries (5oz)	White Salmon Chowder (p.37) & 2 slices of whole wheat bread & Tuscan Style Grilled Octopus (p.52)	Banana Casserole (p.21)	Baked Seabass (p.58) & fresh vegetables (7oz)
24	Salmon Poke Bowl (p.19)	Banana Casserole (p.21)	Tuscan Style Grilled Octopus (p.52) & Greek Roasted Potatoes (p.26) & fresh vegetables (7oz)	Eggs Stuffed with Herring Creamy Pate (p.66)	Salmon Poke Bowl (p.19) & Vegetable Ratatouille (p.28)
25	Whole Grain Pancakes (p.13) & 1 cup Greek yogurt	Eggs Stuffed with Herring Creamy Pate (p.66)	Stuffed Chicken Breast (p.43) & Greek Roasted Potatoes (p.26)	Cold Beet Soup (p.40) & 2 slices of whole wheat bread	Stuffed Chicken Breast (p.43) & Vegetable Ratatouille (p.28)
26	Whole Grain Pancakes (p.13) & 1 cup Greek yogurt	Cashew nuts (1 oz.) and 1 orange	Cold Beet Soup (p.40) & 2 slices of whole wheat bread & Chicken Liver (p.49)	Caprese Skewers (p.66)	Chicken Liver (p.49) & Pesto Pasta (p.26) & Caprese Skewers (p.66)
27	Tuna Salad (p.35) & 2 slices of whole wheat bread	Vanilla Puddings (p.70)	Ukrainian Borsch (p.39) & 2 slices of whole wheat bread & Tuna Salad (p.35)	Vanilla Puddings (p.70)	Salmon Steak with Vegetables (p.57)
28	Blueberry Smoothie Bowl (p.21)	Dry fruits (2 oz.) & cashew nuts (1 oz.)	Ukrainian Borsch (p.39) & 2 slices of whole wheat bread & Citrus Cod Fillet (p.57)	Peach Chia Dessert (p.68)	Salmon Steak with Vegetables (p.57)
29	Salmon Quesadilla (p.20)	Peach Chia Dessert (p.68)	Citrus Cod Fillet (p.57) & Stewed Bulgur (p.25) & fresh vegetables (7oz)	Slices of Apples with Peanut Butter (p.65)	Meatball Curry (p.48) & Stewed Bulgur (p.25) & fresh vegetables (7oz)
30	Buddha Bowl with Quinoa (p.23)	Shrimp Spring Rolls (p. 65)	Meatball Curry (p.48) & Buddha Bowl with Quinoa (p.23)	Shrimp Spring Rolls (p. 65)	Garlic Butter Lobster Tails (p.54) & Udon Noodles

Meal Plan

Day	Breakfast	Mid-Morning Snack	Lunch	Afternoon Snack	Dinner
31	Salmon Wrap (p.16) & cashew nuts (1oz)	Egg and Cheese Muffins (p.63) & 1 cup Greek yogurt	Pasta Farfalle with Seafood (p.61) & fresh vegetables (7oz)	Egg and Cheese Muffins (p. 63) & 1 cup Greek yogurt	Lamb Burgers (p. 51) & fresh vegetables (7oz)
32	Oatmeal with Chicken (p.22)	Egg and Cheese Muffins (p. 63) & 1 cup Greek yogurt	Spicy Pumpkin Soup (p.40) & Lamb Burgers (p. 51)	Fresh berries (5oz)	Pasta Farfalle with Seafood (p.61) & Beet Salad with Orange (p.32)
33	Oatmeal with Chicken (p.22)	Hummus (p.63) & 2 slices of whole wheat bread	Spicy Pumpkin Soup (p.40) & Asian Turkey Meatloaf (p.46) & Beet Salad with Orange (p.32)	Hummus (p.63) & 2 slices of whole wheat bread	Asian Turkey Meatloaf (p.46) & Quinoa Salad (p.33)
34	Chicken Vegetable Bowl (p.32)	Baked Apples (p.72)	Beef and Vegetable Soup (p.38) & Chicken Vegetable Bowl (p.32)	Baked Apples (p.72)	Salmon Steak with Vegetables (p.57) & Quinoa Salad (p.33)
35	Salmon Poke Bowl (p.19)	Creamy Matcha Ice Cream (p.71)	Beef and Vegetable Soup (p.38) & 2 slices of whole wheat bread & Eggplant Boats with Meat (p.44)	Creamy Matcha Ice Cream (p.71)	Salmon Poke Bowl (p.19) & Cauliflower Rice (p.25)
36	Broccoli and Cheese Quiche (p.15)	Sweet Potato Fries with Garlic Aioli (p.62)	Baked Pork (p.45) & whole wheat spaghetti (5 oz cooked) & fresh vegetables (7oz)	Sweet Potato Fries with Garlic Aioli (p.62)	Baked Pork (p.45) & Cauliflower Rice (p.25)
37	Broccoli and Cheese Quiche (p.15)	Blueberry Scones (p.73) & 1 cup Greek yogurt	Pomegranate Glazed Duck Breast (p.41) & Cauliflower Rice Salad (p.34)	Blueberry Scones (p.73) & 1 cup Greek yogurt	Coconut Chicken Curry (p.47) & & brown rice (5oz cooked)
38	Overnight Oats (p.20) & fresh berries (7oz)	Blueberry Scones (p.73)	Pomegranate Glazed Duck Breast (p.41) &brown rice (5oz cooked) & fresh vegetables (7oz)	Slices of Apples with Peanut Butter (p.65)	Salmon Steak with Vegetables (p.57) & Cauliflower Rice Salad (p.34)
39	Turkey Sausage Skillet (p.19) & hazelnuts (1oz)	Guacamole Sandwich (p.64)	Salmon Steak with Vegetables (p.57) & Greek Roasted Potatoes (p.26)	Guacamole Sandwich (p.64)	Stuffed Chicken Breast (p.43) & Greek Roasted Potatoes (p.26)
40	Turkey Sausage Skillet (p.19) & hazelnuts (1oz)	Fresh berries (5oz)	Stuffed Chicken Breast (p.43) & Stewed Bulgur (p.25)	Peach Chia Dessert (p.68)	Chicken Liver (p.49) & Stewed Bulgur (p.25) & fresh vegetables (7oz)
41	Blueberry Smoothie Bowl (p.21)	Peach Chia Dessert (p.68)	Chicken Liver (p.49) & Buddha Bowl with Quinoa (p.23)	Hazelnuts (up to 2oz)	Buddha Bowl with Quinoa (p.23)
42	Grilled Halloumi and Rocket Salad (p.31)	Healthy Dry Turkey Jerky (p.64)	Mediterranean Style Cod (p.55) & Grilled Halloumi and Rocket Salad (p.31)	Healthy Dry Turkey Jerky (p.64)	Mediterranean Style Cod (p.55) & Pesto Pasta (p.26)
43	Steel-cut oats (p.18) & fresh berries	2 Coconut Date Balls (p.73)	Eggplant Boats with Meat (p.44) & Pesto Pasta (p.26)	2 Coconut Date Balls (p.73)	Eggplant Boats with Meat (p.44) & Green Bean Almondine (p.24)
44	Steel-cut oats (p.18) & fresh berries	2 Coconut Date Balls (p.73)	Thai Chicken Satay (p.50) & Green Bean Almondine (p.24)	Cashew nuts (1 oz.) and 1 orange	Thai Chicken Satay (p.50) & Greek Roasted Potatoes (p.26)
45	Sweet Potatoes and Eggs (p.17)	Fresh berries (5oz)	Scallops and Shrimp Delight (p.56) & Greek Roasted Potatoes (p.26)	Baked Cheesecake (p.71)	Scallops and Shrimp Delight (p.56) & Beet Salad with Orange (p.32)

Day	Breakfast	Mid-Morning Snack	Lunch	Afternoon Snack	Dinner
46	Chicken Vegetable Bowl (p.32)	Baked Cheesecake (p.71)	Cold Summer Soup (p.37) & 2 slices of whole wheat bread & Chicken Vegetable Bowl (p.32)	Baked Cheesecake (p.71)	Chicken Strips (p.42) & Beet Salad with Orange (p.32)
47	Whole Grain Pancakes (p.13) & fresh berries	Guacamole Sandwich (p.64)	Cold Summer Soup (p.37) & 2 slices of whole wheat bread & Peach Chia Dessert (p.68)	Hazelnuts (up to 2oz)	Chicken Strips (p.42) & Quinoa Salad (p.33)
48	Whole Grain Pancakes (p.13) & fresh berries	Peach Chia Dessert (p.68)	Meatball Curry (p.48) & Quinoa Salad (p.33)	Slices of Apples with Peanut Butter (p.65)	Meatball Curry (p.48) & Stewed Bulgur (p.25)
49	Apple Quinoa Porridge (p.13)	Slices of Apples with Peanut Butter (p.13)	Sesame Tuna Steaks (p.13) & Stewed Bulgur (p.12)	Egg and Cheese Muffins (p. 41) & 1 cup Greek yogurt	Sesame Tuna Steaks (p.13) & Lemon Herb Couscous (p.12)
50	Apple Quinoa Porridge (p.16)	Egg and Cheese Muffins (p.63) & 1 cup Greek yogurt	Asian Turkey Meatloaf (p.46) & Lemon Herb Couscous (p.29)	Egg and Cheese Muffins (p. 63) & 1 cup Greek yogurt	Asian Turkey Meatloaf (p.46) & Grilled Eggplant (p.24)
51	Broccoli and Cheese Quiche (p.15)	Cashew nuts (1 oz.) and 1 orange	Stir Fry Noodles with Beef (p.50) & Grilled Eggplant (p.24)	Vanilla Puddings (p.70)	Stir Fry Noodles with Beef (p.50) & Grilled Halloumi and Rocket Salad (p, 31)
52	Broccoli and Cheese Quiche (p.15)	Vanilla Puddings (p.70)	Black Bean & Turkey Chili (p.43) & Grilled Halloumi and Rocket Salad (p.31)	1 cup Greek yogurt & fresh berries (5oz)	Black Bean & Turkey Chili (p.43) & fresh vegetables (7oz)
53	Salmon Poke Bowl (p.19)	Banana Casserole (p.21)	Pasta Farfalle with Seafood (p.61) & fresh vegetables (7oz)	Banana Casserole (p.21)	Salmon Poke Bowl (p.19)
54	Turkey Sausage Skillet (p.19) & hazelnuts (1oz)	Eggs Stuffed with Herring Creamy Pate (p.66)	Pasta Farfalle with Seafood (p.61) & Roasted Cauliflower (p.28)	Eggs Stuffed with Herring Creamy Pate (p.66)	Turkey Breast with Oranges (p.51) & Roasted Cauliflower (p.28)
55	Turkey Sausage Skillet (p.19) & hazelnuts (1oz)	Tuna Salad (p.35) & 2 slices of whole wheat bread	Turkey Breast with Oranges (p.51) & Greek Roasted Potatoes (p.26)	Tuna Salad (p.35) & 2 slices of whole wheat bread	Citrus Cod Fillet (p.57) & Greek Roasted Potatoes (p.26)
56	Shrimp and Persimmon Salad (p.35) & 1 cup Greek yogurt	Dry fruits (2 oz.) & cashew nuts (1 oz.)	Citrus Cod Fillet (p.57) & whole wheat spaghetti (5 oz cooked) & fresh vegetables (7oz)	Caprese Skewers (p.66)	Chicken Liver (p.49) & whole wheat spaghetti (5 oz cooked) & Caprese Skewers (p.66)
57	Shrimp and Persimmon Salad (p.34) & 1 cup Greek yogurt	Spicy Sweet Potato (p.27)	Chicken Liver (p.49) & Pesto Pasta (p.26) & fresh vegetables (7oz)	Spicy Sweet Potato (p.27)	Mediterranean Style Cod (p.55) & Pesto Pasta (p.26)
58	Blueberry Smoothie Bowl (p.21)	Peach Chia Dessert (p.68)	Mediterranean Style Cod (p.55) & Quinoa Salad (p.33)	Peach Chia Dessert (p.68)	Stuffed Potato Boats (p.49) & Quinoa Salad (p.33)
59	Overnight Oats (p.20) & fresh berries (7oz)	Hazelnuts (up to 2oz)	Stuffed Potato Boats (p.49) & Stewed Bulgur (p.25)	Guacamole Sandwich (p.64)	Baked Pork (p.45) & Stewed Bulgur (p.25) & fresh vegetables (7oz)
60	Buddha Bowl with Quinoa (p.26)	Baked Apples (p.72)	Baked Pork (p.45) & Buddha Bowl with Quinoa (p.26)	Baked Apples (p.72)	Pasta Farfalle with Seafood (p.61) & fresh vegetables (7oz)

Made in the USA
Coppell, TX
08 September 2024

36965687R00044